ANY LAST WORDS?

For permission requests, please contact the publisher at:
Mango Publishing Group
2850 S Douglas Road, 2nd Floor
Coral Gables, FL 33134 USA
info@mango.bz

For special orders, quantity sales, course adoptions and corporate
sales, please email the publisher at sales@mango.bz. For trade and
wholesale sales, please contact Ingram Publisher Services at customer.
service@ingramcontent.com or +1.800.509.4887.

Any Last Words?: Deathbed Quotes and Famous Farewells

Library of Congress Cataloging-in-Publication number: 2019938544
ISBN: (print) 978-1-63353-990-7, (ebook) 978-1-63353-991-4
BISAC category code: HUM015000—HUMOR / Form / Anecdotes &
Quotations

Printed in the United States of America

ANY LAST WORDS?

Deathbed Quotes and Famous Farewells

JOSEPH HAYDEN

CORAL GABLES

Disclaimer

This book is not meant as an academic work. While the information herein is thought to be common knowledge, that does not necessarily make it true, nor has it been peer-reviewed. Furthermore, none of the speakers of these last words have been available for comment, due to a mortality rate of 100 percent. Please accept this as a work meant purely for entertainment, though hopefully it will inspire readers to seek out the truth about these (mostly) great people.

TABLE OF CONTENTS

INTRODUCTION

Your last words are probably the hardest you will ever say.
First of all, you are almost certain to be in the worst health of
your life. If you are lucky enough to be in a hospital at a ripe
old age, surrounded by friends and family, you are likely to
be distracted by being really, really sick. If you die suddenly,
anything other than "Ugggh" can be seen as a win. Outside
of the fortunate few, these last words are rarely the ones of
serene, calm individuals.

However, despite the fact that final words aren't always the
most eloquent, they are significant. They are often a little
glimpse into the speaker: a snapshot of a person's truest self.
Other times they are examples of people reacting to the most
difficult situations they will ever face. Some are clever, others
are loving, some are heartbreaking, a few are desperately sad,
but all say something about the speaker.

In these pages you will find the last words of over two
hundred actors, writers, musicians, politicians, criminals,
thinkers, athletes, and more. We will look at a brief snapshot
of each of these extraordinary lives and the ways in which
many of their final words provided a fitting epitaph to a life
interestingly lived.

It is worth repeating that none of the speakers involved have responded to requests for authentication or clarification, so we will have to make our best guesses as to the true intention of each. As for the words themselves, some have been passed down through centuries, others were recorded by dubious sources, and all are to be taken with at least a pinch of salt—though many of the most beautiful truths can be found in fabrications.

CHAPTER ONE

HOLLYWOOD

Hollywood has been built on the phenomenal talents of men and women like Charlie Chaplin, John Wayne, and Marilyn Monroe—all of whom are now dead. Stanley Kubrick is also dead, and so are Mary Pickford and Peter Sellers. Alfred Hitchcock, Groucho Marx, Joan Crawford? Dead, dead, and dead. Death comes to us all, even the famous and beautiful. These are people who left an unmistakable mark on the world, people whose work has inspired generations, and people who are now super-duper dead. Have you ever wondered why Paul Newman hasn't made a film in a while? I will give you one guess.

All of these talented superstars have left behind a legacy. To paraphrase Robin Williams quoting Walt Whitman in *Dead Poets Society*, the powerful play goes on, and they have contributed a verse. A few of them were even able to sneak in one more great line before the end. From the hilarious to the heartfelt, here are a few of the best last lines of some of Hollywood's brightest stars.

GROUCHO MARX (1890–1977)

It would be hard to find a modern comedian who wasn't influenced by Groucho Marx. One of the quickest and most quotable wits in the history of Hollywood, Groucho lines have become a part of everyday life. The man with the bushy black moustache and ubiquitous cigar made thirteen films with the Marx brothers, including the classic *Duck Soup*, as well as enjoying decades of success as a solo act on radio, screen, and stage, including the hit show *You Bet Your Life*.

His impact is so broad that even Queen Elizabeth II quoted him on her eightieth birthday, saying "Anyone can get old—all you have to do is live long enough."

Only someone as clever as Groucho would have too many good lines to settle on just one final zinger. A few close friends have suggested that his last words were "This is no way to live!" while most suggest that his last words were to his wife, specifically:

"Die, my dear? Why, that's the last thing I'll do!"

Either way, everyone agrees that Groucho left with one heck of a one-liner.

CHARLIE CHAPLIN (1889–1977)

Chaplin was one of Hollywood's first true auteurs. He did everything. He acted, directed, produced, and wrote. He even recorded the soundtracks for his films. He was a perfectionist and it shows. His films are still loved almost a century later, and his Tramp character has become a film icon.

Though he was known best for his silent films, such as *City Lights* and *Modern Times*, Chaplin had a rapier wit, even on his deathbed. After a priest had read him his rites, ending on "May the Lord have mercy on your soul," Chaplin chimed in:

"Why not? After all, it belongs to him."

BOB HOPE (1903–2003)

Hope lived to be one hundred years old, and, in true Bob Hope style, he used this as fodder for a one-liner, famously musing, "You know you're getting old when the candles cost more than the cake."

From his first films in the mid-1930s to his last USO tours in the early 1990s, Bob Hope was a ubiquitous presence on American stage and screen. He appeared in more than sixty films, including the famous Road movies with Bing Crosby. He hosted the Academy Awards nineteen times, and he golfed with eleven presidents—including one notable occasion when he rounded out a foursome with Ford, Clinton, and Bush.

It is safe to say he had pretty much seen it all in his century as an actor, singer, dancer, golfer, comedian, host, USO performer, and all-around entertainer. So his last words were fitting indeed:

"Surprise me."

BING CROSBY (1903–1977)

The other half of the road-movie duo, Bing, was truly one of a kind. His awards list includes an Oscar, three stars on the Hollywood Walk of Fame, a Cecil B. DeMille Award, and the first ever Grammy Lifetime Achievement Award. He was a beloved actor, and he had a voice that has inspired generations of crooners and set a bar for Christmas carols that still hasn't been beat.

To say that Crosby was an American institution would be an understatement. He was in the top ten for box-office sales for fifteen years, while also managing to record twenty-three albums that went gold or platinum. He did it all with an approachable, nice-guy image that resonated with pretty much everyone on earth, and still does to this day.

Crosby died doing what he loved. After playing a round of golf in Spain, a game he reportedly lost by one stroke, Bing suffered a massive heart attack on his way back to the clubhouse. His last words:

"That was a great game of golf, fellas."

JOSEPHINE BAKER (1906–1975)

Baker did it all. She was an actor, singer, dancer, writer, activist, and French Resistance agent. She lived in a castle, spoke at marches alongside Martin Luther King Jr., and was awarded medals for her part in World War II.

At age sixty-eight, she was starring in a retrospective of her work in Paris, a show attended by Mick Jagger, Diana Ross, and Liza Minelli. A couple of days after the show, she died of a cerebral hemorrhage and was found at her home, surrounded by clippings of rave reviews. The last words anyone remembers her saying were as she left a party in her honor:

"Oh, you young people act like old men. You are no fun."

JOHN BARRYMORE (1882–1942)

John was born into a theatrical family, a family that he would propel to new heights as one of the early stars of the screen. While Barrymore first rose to fame on the stage, taking on some of Shakespeare's most famous roles, he was best known for his light comedies and charming on-screen demeanor. Due to a combination of his famous good looks and stage-trained voice, he was one of the most successful actors during the transition from silent films to talkies.

He was also perhaps the first bad boy of Hollywood. His famous quips include, "You can only be as good as you dare to be bad," and "Sex: the thing that takes up the least amount of time and causes the most amount of trouble." His last words:

"Die? I should say not, dear fellow. No Barrymore would allow such a conventional thing to happen to him."

JOAN CRAWFORD (1905–1977)

In the 1930s, Joan Crawford quickly moved from being Hollywood's "It Girl" to being Hollywood's "It Woman." She played characters that were as smart, hardworking, and as tough as she was, and boy was she tough. Crawford famously butted heads with just about everyone in the business and had a legendary rivalry with Bette Davis.

One of Crawford's most famous lines is, "You have to be self-reliant and strong to survive in this town. Otherwise you will be destroyed." And nobody lived this credo like Joan.

Crawford's sharp tongue and fierce independence never faltered, even at the end. In Joan's last moments, her maid dropped to her knees to pray by her bedside, but Crawford cut the pleas short:

"Damn it! Don't you dare ask God to help me!"

DONALD O'CONNOR (1925–2003)

An incredibly prolific star of stage, film, and television, O'Connor is perhaps better known for his supporting roles than for his many leads. The talented song-and-dance man had a lot of memorable moments in a lot of great films, but the one he is best known for is his award-winning role as Cosmo Brown in *Singin' in the Rain*, which features his hilarious performance of "Make 'Em Laugh."

Despite his impressive list of credits, O'Connor has been called one of the most underrated stars of his era. On his deathbed, he joked to his family:

"I'd like to thank the Academy for my lifetime achievement award that I will eventually get."

(Sadly, he has yet to receive it.)

DOUGLAS FAIRBANKS (1883–1939)

The swashbuckling star of silent films such as *Robin Hood* and *The Mark of Zorro* was at one time known as the king of Hollywood. Fairbanks shone in the era of silent films, becoming the epitome of a matinee movie star with his many turns as lovable costumed rogues, pirates, thieves, and outlaws.

In the 1920s, his stardom went through the stratosphere when he married Mary Pickford. The pair are commonly recognized as Hollywood's first power couple and were met by legions of adoring fans everywhere they went.

Sadly, Fairbanks's time at the top was short, as his health and fame declined during the talkie era, and he and Pickford separated in the mid-1930s. He died in 1939 of a heart attack at his home. His last words:

"I've never felt better."

SIR LAURENCE OLIVIER (1907–1989)

There is perhaps no other actor that has had the combined impact on both stage and screen as Sir Laurence Olivier. Olivier dominated the West End, helped build the Old Vic into the respected company it is today, and was the founding director of Britain's National Theatre. He then went on to star in more than fifty films, as well as several television shows.

While Olivier played all kinds of roles, he is best known for his work as a Shakespearean actor. Sir Laurence played every great role the Bard ever put to paper. Being a thespian was so ingrained in Olivier's DNA that Shakespeare inspired his final words. On his deathbed, when a nurse who was trying to moisten his lips got overzealous with the water, Olivier rebuked her, saying:

"This isn't *Hamlet*, you know. It's not meant to go into the bloody ear."

MARILYN MONROE (1926–1962)

Perhaps nobody has broken as many hearts as the blonde bombshell, Marilyn Monroe. This gifted actress solidified her place at the top of the Hollywood it-list with star turns in films like *Gentlemen Prefer Blondes* and *Some Like It Hot*.

Marilyn herself was the subject of the last words of Joe DiMaggio.

The night before she died, she talked to Ratpacker and JFK brother-in-law Peter Lawford and said:

"Say goodbye to Pat, say goodbye to Jack, and say goodbye to yourself, because you're a nice guy."

ALFRED HITCHCOCK (1899–1980)

There is no question that Hitchcock is one of the greatest directors of all time. Even though he, amazingly, never won an Oscar for directing, he created a list of masterpieces that is unrivalled in his genre: *Psycho*, *Rear Window*, *Vertigo*, *The Birds*, *North by Northwest*, *Rebecca*, and the list goes on and on.

His impact can't be overstated. There is no other director that can be named just at the appearance of his shadow or upon the sound of his theme music.

The king of thrillers had more than a few things to say about the nature of film and life, including "Drama is life with the dull bits cut out," and "There is no terror in the bang, only in the anticipation of it." While they weren't quite his very last words, in his last days Hitchcock left us with one more memorable line:

"One never knows the ending. One has to die to know exactly what happens after death. Although Catholics have their hopes."

DEL CLOSE (1934–1999)

Del Close was of the key figures in the rise of improvisational theatre. Along with his longtime collaborators Charna Halpern and David Shepherd, Close helped to propel the American improv scene to new heights. Through the '80s and '90s, his teaching and guidance affected the comedy world more than perhaps any other single person.

Close's students included Bill Murray, Chris Farley, Gilda Radner, John Candy, Stephen Colbert, Harold Ramis, John Belushi, Bob Odenkirk, Tina Fey, Mike Myers, and Amy Poehler—and that is just an abridged list to save space. His impact is still felt on the stages of New York, Chicago, and beyond.

His physical presence is still felt at Chicago's Goodman Theatre, as in his will Close bequeathed his skull to the theater with instructions that it was to be used in *Hamlet* and that he should be credited in the program for playing Yorick. Funny to the end, Close's last words were:

"I'm tired of being the funniest one in the room."

HUMPHREY BOGART (1899–1957)

By all accounts, Bogart earned his tough-guy reputation. He was thrown out of private school (it is rumored for throwing his headmaster into a pond), served in the Navy, and honed his craft through hard-nosed persistence. After years of paying his dues, Bogart's hard work paid off with star turns in classic films such as *Casablanca*, *The Caine Mutiny*, *The African Queen*, and *The Maltese Falcon*.

There are two different lines that have been reported to be the last words of Hollywood's favorite tough guy. Some say Bogie's last words were, "I should never have switched from Scotch to martinis." These certainly sound like the hard-nosed actor we all know and love from his films. However, his wife Lauren Bacall reports that Bogart's actual last words were a bit more touching, though still in character. As Bacall was leaving Bogie's bedside to pick up their children, he said:

"Goodbye, kid. Hurry back."

TALLULAH BANKHEAD (1902–1968)

Tallulah Bankhead isn't a household name, but she should be, as anyone who has seen her fantastic turn in Hitchcock's film *Lifeboat* will tell you. Known as much for her caustic wit and devil-may-care attitude as for her impressive skills on the stage and screen, Bankhead was well ahead of her time.

Bankhead's more famous witticisms include, "If I had to live my life again, I'd make the same mistakes, only sooner" and "Only good girls keep diaries. Bad girls don't have time."

She was unapologetic about her vices, famously drinking many a man under the table. Bankhead died at sixty-six, catching pneumonia after hanging out backstage in the nude. Her last words:

"Codeine, bourbon."

CHARLES GUSSMAN (1913–2000)

Like Tallulah, Gussman also may not be a household name. He made his mark behind the scenes as a writer of radio and television serials and soap operas. Gussman's radio credits include *Young Doctor Malone*, *The Right to Happiness*, and *The Road of Life*. In later years he contributed to television shows, including *Gilligan's Island* and the soap opera *Days of Our Lives*, the latter of which he is credited with naming.

While Gussman gave a lot of well-timed lines to a lot of characters over the years, he saved the best one for himself. On his deathbed, with his daughter at his side, Gussman reportedly leaned over and, with his last breath, said:

"And now for a final word from our sponsor."

WALT DISNEY (1901-1966)

There is no question that Walt Disney's combination of imagination and business sense changed the world. Regardless of what you think about today's juggernaut of a corporation, Disney set the bar for animated films and created theme parks that, to this day, fill the dreams of children of all ages. As Walt himself once said, "All our dreams can come true, if we only have the courage to pursue them."

Walt Disney Studios has been a launching pad for countless actors over the years: Shia LeBeouf, Ryan Gosling, that guy from the *John Carter* movie, Hillary Duff, and Kurt Russell, to name a few, though it is the last one that is important here. Apparently, as Walt was breathing his last, it wasn't Mary Poppins or Mickey Mouse that filled his thoughts, but rather Snake Plissken. Just before his death, Disney wrote a note on a piece of paper. It said:

"Kurt Russell."

JAMES STEWART (1908–1997)

There are two types of people in this world: those who are fans of Jimmy Stewart and those you are better off not knowing.

The star of such films as *Vertigo*, *It's A Wonderful Life*, and *Harvey* also flew missions for the US Air Force in World

War II and had a fascinating life-long best friendship with Henry Fonda.

He is probably best summed up by this famous line from Harvey: " 'In this world, Elwood, you must be oh so smart, or oh so pleasant.' For years I was smart. I recommend pleasant."

Stewart lost his wife a few years before his own death, and his last thoughts were of her. His last words:

"I'm going to go be with Gloria now."

STAN LAUREL (1890–1965)

Stan is best known as the thin one in the legendary duo Laurel and Hardy. The pair were a phenomenon in their early slapstick films and only got funnier when they transitioned to talkies. The duo appeared in more than a hundred films together, including twenty-three features.

Laurel was often the head writer of the duo's sketches and was known to have an extremely quick wit, both on and off stage. He was renowned for playing pranks and running sketches every chance he got.

On his deathbed, Laurel told his nurse "I'd rather be skiing," which prompted her to ask if he knew how to ski. His reply:

"No, but I'd rather be skiing than doing what I'm doing."

OLIVER HARDY (1892–1957)

Hardy died eight years before his partner. While the larger half of the pair was often the idea man on screen, he was actually the more laid-back half of the duo in real life. Known to his friends as Babe, Hardy was a gentle giant, well-liked by all who knew him.

Ollie is perhaps best known for his delivery of the line, "Well, here's another nice mess you've gotten me into," that often punctuated Laurel and Hardy's sketches.

His last years were beset by health problems, including heart attacks and strokes, the first of which hit him during his final tour with Laurel. He died with his wife by his side. His last words were to her:

"I love you."

LUCILLE BALL (1911–1989)

The titular star of *I Love Lucy* did it all. She was an outrageously funny comedian, a talented actress, a model, a producer, and a studio executive. They had to build new glass ceilings just so she could break through them.

Lucy left us with a lot of fantastic lines like, "The secret of staying young is to live honestly, eat slowly, and lie about your age," and "A man who correctly guesses a woman's age may be smart, but he isn't very bright." Her final words were simple, but strangely haunting. In response to a nurse asking her if there was anything she needed, Lucy answered:

"My Florida water."

DESI ARNAZ (1917-1986)

It is impossible to think of Lucy without thinking of her on- and off-stage love, Desi Arnaz. Like his famous wife, the Cuban-born actor and musician broke down many barriers of his own. Desi managed to become not only a national star but also an important voice behind the scenes as a cofounder of Desilu Productions, while never losing touch with his heritage or resorting to easy humor.

Though the couple had some decidedly rocky times, ultimately divorcing in 1960, they remained fast friends until Desi's death. In fact, Desi's last words, before he finally lost his long battle with lung cancer, were reportedly spoken over the phone to his ex-wife:

"I love you too, honey. Good luck with your show."

CHAPTER TWO

WRITERS

For those whose entire lives are about leaving their mark on the annals of history, one would think that last words are especially crucial. As Mark Twain famously pointed out, "The difference between the almost right word and the right word is really a large matter—it's the difference between the lightning bug and the lightning."

It should come as no surprise then that many of the writers listed in this chapter were indeed prepared for their one shot at nailing that all-important last line—though others, including Twain himself, seemingly found themselves with a very untimely case of writer's block.

VOLTAIRE (1694–1778)

To say that Voltaire was prolific would be like saying that the Eiffel Tower is somewhat well-known. The French playwright, novelist, poet, essayist, pamphleteer, historian, and academic wrote more than twenty thousand letters and more than two thousand books and pamphlets. Even more impressively, a lot of them are actually pretty good.

Voltaire was known for his lifelong battle against censorship, a battle that landed him in prison on a couple of occasions, including a stint in the Bastille and, worse yet, exile in England. There was no topic too high to be a target for his sharp tongue.

Many of his quotes have become commonplace sayings, such as, "Those who can make you believe absurdities can make you commit atrocities," "Common sense is not so common," and "Judge of a man by his questions rather than by his answers."

Another of Voltaire's best-known quotes is "A witty saying proves nothing," which is somewhat ironic considering his last words. When Voltaire was asked on his deathbed to renounce Satan, he answered:

"Now is the not the time for making new enemies."

Dylan Thomas (1914–1953)

Thomas would top most lists of famous Welshmen. In his thirty-nine short years, Thomas managed to write some of the world's most beloved and well-known poems and had an illustrious career in radio.

He was also one of history's most famous drinkers. He saw it as more a point of honor than a hindrance, and, by all accounts, he could do it better than most. One of the poet's most famous quotes sums up his feelings on the matter: "An alcoholic is someone you don't like who drinks as much as you do."

Thomas himself did not go gentle into that good night; he did not go gentle at all. In fact, his last days involved staying at the infamous Hotel Chelsea and doing a fair bit of drinking. The night before he died, Thomas famously returned from the pub and announced:

"I've had eighteen straight whiskies. I think that's the record!"

EMILY DICKINSON (1830–1886)

One of America's greatest poets, Dickinson lived most of her life in isolation. Her few relationships survived through correspondence, and correspond she could. Dickinson was one of the most beautiful writers who ever to put pen to paper. Her best-loved lines include "To live is so startling it leaves little time for anything else" and "Beauty is not caused. It is."

The end of her life was fraught with sadness, as she lost what seemed like an endless stream of friends and family, one after another, until she finally lost her own years-long battle with Bright's disease. Her last words were as haunting as one might expect:

"I must go in, for the fog is rising."

OSCAR WILDE (1854–1900)

Wilde was, and perhaps still is, the undisputed master of witticisms. The beloved writer of plays, novels, essays, and heartbreaking children's stories has left more memorable lines in his wake than anyone not born in Stratford-upon-Avon.

It is fitting that Wilde was as prolific on his deathbed as he was throughout his life. In his final days, Wilde left us with a bevy of lines that only he could deliver, and, while none of them were his absolute final ones, all of them are memorable. They include:

"I am dying beyond my means," "It would really be more than the English could stand if another century began and I were still alive," and "My wallpaper and I are fighting a duel to the death. One or the other of us has to go."

Henrik Ibsen (1828–1906)

Ibsen was a Norwegian playwright who influenced basically every playwright of the twentieth century. To give some sense of how beloved Ibsen was by some of his contemporaries, James Joyce reportedly became fluent in Norwegian just so he could read Ibsen in his original language.

Known as the father of realism, Ibsen has a dark humor that runs through much of his work, which was on full display in his final hour.

In his last days, Ibsen was bedridden after suffering from a stroke. Just before he died, an acquaintance who had come to visit asked about his health, and Ibsen's nurse suggested that the writer was on the mend. Ibsen's reply and last words were:

"On the contrary."

Ian Fleming (1908–1964)

The author of all of the James Bond novels that are worth reading, Fleming's own life reflected that of 007 more than one might expect. Fleming was an intelligence officer during World War II and was involved in planning Operation Goldeneye. He excelled at athletics, attended a tiny private school run by a former British spy, and had several broken engagements and affairs with high-profile women.

Though he was not a strong English student as a young man, Fleming eventually went on to a fairly successful career as a journalist and a wildly successful career as a novelist, writing not only the Bond novels, but also the children's favorite *Chitty Chitty Bang Bang*.

Sadly, Fleming's heavy smoking and hard drinking led to a series of ailments which cut his life short. His last words were to paramedics who were transporting him to the hospital following a heart attack. He was politely British to the end:

"I am sorry to trouble you chaps. I don't know how you get along so fast with the traffic on the roads these days."

LOUISA MAY ALCOTT (1832–1888)

Most will know Alcott from her *Little Women*, a loose recollection of her own childhood that has withstood the test of time and become a children's favorite. Fewer know that the American-born novelist and poet was a revolutionary.

Alcott grew up learning from and speaking with intellectuals such as Henry David Thoreau and Ralph Waldo Emerson.

She and her family helped escaped slaves navigating the Underground Railroad, even housing Frederick Douglass. As well as an active abolitionist, Louisa May was a staunch feminist, remaining independent throughout her life.

Alcott's health deteriorated in her later years, despite her being an avid runner which went against the gender norms of the time. In the end, it took some combination of typhoid fever—which she contracted during her service in the American Civil War—mercury poisoning from the treatment, and perhaps lupus to take her down, and, even then, she thought she could beat it. Her last words:

"Is it not meningitis?"

WILLIAM S. BURROUGHS (1914–1997)

The elder statesman of the Beat Generation, Burroughs was a writer, traveler, and famous user of narcotics. Burroughs divides critics like few others. His works range from linear stories involving heavy drug use to psychedelic narratives that some found impenetrable. While some saw Burroughs as an important counterculture voice, others fought to ban his works for obscenity. The author was as equally as contentious as his work. His well-documented drug and alcohol use sadly contributed to a William Tell stunt gone wrong which resulted in the accidental shooting of his common-law wife, Joan Vollmer.

Perhaps the most surprising aspect of Burroughs's life is that he lived to the ripe old age of eighty-four. Burroughs had a hand in many of the counterculture movements of the twentieth century, including the Beat Generation in the 1950s and Andy Warhol's Factory in the 1960s and 1970s.

Despite years of heavy drug use (he was still an active heroin user in his eighties), in the end Burroughs died near his small house in Kansas, of a heart attack on the way to the store. His last words:

"Back in no time."

HERMAN MELVILLE (1819–1891)

Melville is best known for writing *Moby Dick*, a novel that often finishes the sentences "One day I mean to read..." and "I should really finish..." While the novel is a favorite bookshelf filler for today's well-meaning fans of the classics, it was not well received until long after Melville's death.

It took even longer for people to appreciate *Billy Budd*, a novel that was left unfinished after Melville's death but was finally published more than thirty years later, in 1924. Melville's last words suggest that at least he thought it might be something of a success, as he died referencing one of the novel's characters:

"God Bless Captain Vere!"

JANE AUSTEN (1775–1817)

Jane Austen only published four novels in her lifetime and two more posthumously. This means that her film-adaptation-to-novel ratio is somewhere in the neighborhood of ten thousand to one.

Austen's name never appeared on the covers of her novels during her lifetime. *Sense and Sensibility* was credited as being written "By A Lady," and all subsequent novels were billed as being by the author of *Sense and Sensibility*.

Austen died at age forty-one of a combination of Addison's disease and Hodgkin's lymphoma. At first, she apologized for her illness, making light of it and seeing it as weakness in herself, but, by the end of a long hard fight, she was sadly ready to go:

"I want nothing but death."

SIR ARTHUR CONAN DOYLE (1859–1930)

Conan Doyle is almost as interesting as the characters he created. The writer was a doctor, a botanist, a sailor, an adventurer, an amateur architect, and a politician. He even studied the occult and mysticism. And, amidst all this, he still found time to create the many adventures of Sherlock Holmes.

Conan Doyle was also something of a sportsman. He boxed, played goalkeeper in soccer, and was on an amateur cricket team that also featured A. A. Milne and J. M. Barrie.

After his first wife died of tuberculosis, he married Jean Elizabeth Leckie, who became the love of his life. When he died in his garden of a heart attack at age seventy-one, his last words were to her:

"You are wonderful."

EUGENE O'NEILL (1888–1953)

The Pulitzer Prize–winning playwright of *The Ice Man Cometh* and *Long Day's Journey into Night*, among other works, Eugene O'Neill was known as one of the great realist American writers.

The characters in his works often suffer from pessimism and disillusionment and ultimately end in tragedy and despair, a bleak outlook that was also attributed to O'Neill's own life, with some validity. While his works might have been dark, his writing was often beautiful. O'Neill was known for his combination of wit and introspection, which is seen in many of his best-known quotes, such as "Man's loneliness is but his fear of life," and "Obsessed by a fairy tale, we spend our lives searching for a magic door and a lost kingdom of peace."

O'Neill's dark wit was on full display as he passed away in a hotel room in Boston, sixty-five years after being born in a hotel in Manhattan:

"I knew it! I knew it! Born in a hotel room and, God damn it, died in a hotel room."

ROD SERLING (1924–1975)

Serling is best known as the creative force behind *The Twilight Zone*. He created, hosted, and produced the classic science fiction anthology series, as well as writing a whopping ninety-two episodes.

While radio and television audiences of the 1950s and 1960s loved him, the name Serling filled censors and producers with fear. Dubbed the angry young man of Hollywood, Serling spent his career fighting censorship and discussing hot-button topics such as racism, sexism, and war. Serling was a strong critic of the latter following his decorated service in World War II, which included a Purple Heart and a Bronze Star medal.

At only fifty years old, after years of smoking up to four packs a day, Serling suffered a series of heart attacks over the course of a couple of weeks. True to his prolific career, Serling had not one, but two famous last lines. His last spoken words were "That's what I anticipate death will be: a totally unconscious void in which you float through eternity with no particular consciousness about anything." Later, while unable to speak, he wrote a final note to a friend at his bedside. It said:

"You can't kill this tough Jew."

APHRA BEHN (1640–1689)

The first Englishwoman to earn a living as a writer, Behn was famously mysterious. Nobody knows for certain who her parents were, where she came from, or if her real name was even Aphra Behn. This isn't because this information is lost to the annals of time; it's because she was as secretive as a spy—which makes sense, because she likely worked as an actual spy for King Charles. What we do know for sure is that Behn wrote some truly fantastic plays, nineteen in all, as well as some of the best poetry and prose of the era.

Virginia Woolf famously wrote of Behn: "All women together ought to let flowers fall upon the tomb of Aphra Behn which is, most scandalously but rather appropriately, in Westminster Abbey, for it was she who earned them the right to speak their minds."

While we can't be certain of Behn's last words, we do know the words that are inscribed on her tombstone:

"Here lies a Proof that Wit can never be Defence enough against Mortality."

VLADIMIR NABOKOV (1899–1977)

You know those long Russian novels that feature a bunch of tragedy with too many characters and too much going on? That was the real life of Vladimir Nabokov. His family fled Russia during the revolution, his father died jumping in front of an assassin's bullet meant for a political colleague, his sister got Ayn Rand into politics, his brother was killed by the Nazis, he taught literature to Supreme Court Justice Ruth Bader Ginsburg, and, somewhere in all of this, he wrote a boatload of great novels, stories, poetry, and plays in both Russian and English.

The greatest of his novels is *Lolita*, which was later turned into an outstanding film by Stanley Kubrick. Yet it is suggested that Nabokov's true love was entomology and more specifically lepidopterology—his collection of male blue butterfly genitalia can still be found at the Harvard Museum of Natural History.

It was this love of butterflies that was apparently on Nabokov's mind when he died. His last words were:

"A certain butterfly is already on the wing."

MARK TWAIN (1835–1910)

While the 1897 reports of Twain's death may have been greatly exaggerated, he did eventually die almost exactly when he hoped to. "I came in with Halley's Comet in 1835. It is coming again next year, and I expect to go out with it. It will be the greatest disappointment of my life if I don't go out with Halley's Comet." America's greatest writer died one day after the comet's 1910 return.

As luck would have it, the Halley's Comet prediction wasn't the only portentous thing Mark Twain wrote about death. In a piece about last words for the *Buffalo Express* in 1889, Twain wrote, "A distinguished man should be as particular about his last words as he is about his last breath. He should write them out on a slip of paper and take the judgment of his friends on them." Later in the same piece, he goes on to add: "There is hardly a case on record where a man came to his last moment unprepared and said a good thing, hardly a case where a man trusted to that last moment and did not make a solemn botch of it and go out of the world feeling absurd."

Twain's own last words were indeed written on a piece of paper, but they were likely not quite as distinguished as he may have hoped, although it is almost certain he would have found humor in that. As he lay dying, too tired to speak, he wrote this to his daughter, Clara, who was at his bedside:

"Give me my glasses."

WILLIAM SHAKESPEARE (1564–1616)

Sadly, we do not know the actual last words of the world's greatest writer, though he did write several of the most memorable last lines ever put to page. So, in place of his own, let's look at some of the great last lines from characters in a few of the Bard's most beloved works.

HAMLET

"The rest is silence."

JULIUS CAESAR

"*Et tu, Brute!* Then fall, Caesar!"

MACBETH

"Lay on, Macduff,
And damn'd be him that first cries, 'Hold, enough!' "

OTHELLO

"I kiss'd thee ere I kill'd thee: no way but this;
Killing myself, to die upon a Kiss."

KING RICHARD III

"A horse! A horse! My kingdom for a horse!"

CLEOPATRA

"What should I stay..."

MERCUTIO

"A plague o' both your houses!"

They have made worms' meat of me: I have it, And soundly too: your houses!"

ROMEO

"O true apothecary!
Thy drugs are quick. Thus, with a kiss, I die."

JULIET

"Yea, noise? Then I'll be brief. O happy dagger!
This is thy sheath;
there rust, and let me die."

KING LEAR

"And my poor fool is hang'd! No, no, no life!

Why should a dog, a horse, a rat, have life,

And thou no breath at all? Thou'lt come no more, Never, never, never, never, never!

Pray you, undo this button: thank you, sir.

Do you see this? Look on her, look, her lips, Look there, look there!"

CHAPTER THREE

Politicians and Leaders

As John Donne famously wrote, "Death comes equally to us all and makes us all equal when it comes." Whether you are a prince or a pauper, even those who manage to evade taxes can't escape death. For some of us, this is a nice reminder that the people yelling at each other on the TV aren't so special, but, for the folks in charge, it is a grim reminder that even the mighty will fall. And fall they do.

The one part Donne was wrong about, however, is that we are all equal when death comes knocking. The difference between Joe Coffeeshop and a world leader is that nobody is writing down what Joe says before his last breath. For many great leaders, this is the one time when their words won't have repercussions. Their one chance to drop the facade they have to show the world and truly be themselves, whether they mean to or not.

BENJAMIN FRANKLIN (1706–1790)

Franklin is probably the most famous founding father that never went on to be president or inspire a Broadway musical. An academic, abolitionist, journalist, publisher, library founder, lightning harnesser, musician, postmaster, penny-pincher, oceanographer, inventor, meteorologist, anthropologist, author, ambassador, and turkey aficionado, Franklin deserves his place on the hundred-dollar bill. When it comes to founding America, it is truly all about the Benjamins.

While Franklin authored many famous quotes that have withstood the test of time, such as "Early to bed and early to rise makes a man healthy, wealthy and wise," and "By failing to prepare, you are preparing to fail," his final words haven't seeped into the collective consciousness, but they are certainly no less true:

"Dying men can do nothing easy."

SIR WINSTON CHURCHILL (1874–1965)

One of the world's most memorable leaders, the man best known for leading Great Britain during World War II lived a lot of life in his ninety years.

On top of his well-documented life in the realms of politics and the military, Churchill did more in his spare time than most of us do in a lifetime. He crashed a plane, escaped a prison camp in Cuba, owned a large menagerie of animals, and was both an accomplished amateur painter and a prolific and well-respected writer—so respected, in fact, that he won the Nobel Prize for Literature in 1953.

After spending the better part of nine decades at the forefront of history, it is no surprise that Churchill was exhausted by the end. His last words came just before he slipped into a coma that he would never wake from:

"I'm bored with it all."

MARIE ANTOINETTE (1755–1793)

The last queen of France and famous suggester of the eating of cakes (though there is no record of her actually having said the famous phrase), Antoinette lived a famously fancy life. Have you seen the Palace of Versailles? But, in the end, she was hoisted with her own gold-plated and jewel-encrusted petard.

Though it should be pointed out that, for all of her faults, even Marie's detractors agreed that she was a good mother and was brave and poised in the face of death. This poise could be seen right up to her last moment. Her last words came as she was making her way to the guillotine and accidentally stepped on the executioner's foot.

"Pardonnez-moi, monsieur. Je ne l'ai pas fait exprès."

("Excuse me, sir. I did not do it on purpose.")

CHE GUEVARA (1928–1967)

If you know the name of one revolutionary, this is probably it. Ernesto "Che" Guevara's path from the idealistic medical student who wrote *The Motorcycle Diaries* to the violent revolutionary who penned *Guerrilla Warfare* is fascinating. Whether or not you agree with his politics or ideals, there is no denying his charisma and lasting appeal as a symbol of revolution. If you don't believe me, just look at the T-shirts and posters in any college dorm room.

After successfully helping Fidel Castro to power in Cuba, Guevara traveled the world looking to aid other like-minded revolutions. His path ended in Bolivia, where he was captured and executed. Even in his final moments, his thoughts were with the lasting impact of the revolution:

"I know you've come to kill me. Shoot, coward! You are only going to kill a man!"

ALEXANDER HAMILTON (1755–1804)

The ten-dollar founding father without a father was certainly not throwing away his shot.

The world will never be the same as it was before he blew us all away. Unfortunately, he failed to talk less and smile more and died at the hands of Aaron Burr, sir, even though he had followed the ten duel commandments.

While Hamilton's last words in Lin-Manuel Miranda's fantastic musical are "Raise a glass to freedom," according to those who were in the room where it happened, Hamilton's actual last words were:

"Remember, my Eliza, you are a Christian."

PETER THE GREAT (1672-1725)

Peter I officially became Tsar of Russia when he was ten years old. Over the next forty or so years, he expanded the Russian Empire, spearheaded a cultural revolution inspired by the Enlightenment, and fathered fourteen children.

Only three of his children outlived him, and one of those only did so by a few months. Making matters of succession trickier, none of his surviving heirs were male. So, when he reached for a pen and paper on his deathbed with the intent of penning his final will and testament, it must have been of great interest to all in the room. Unfortunately, all he managed to write was:

"Leave all to..."

THOMAS DE MAHY, MARQUIS DE FAVRAS (1744–1790)

The Marquis de Favras was a soldier and a royalist who was involved in a plot to save King Louis XVI and end the French Revolution.

Unfortunately for Favras, he confided his plan to the wrong people and, after a questionable trial, was sentenced to death by hanging.

While all of this is noteworthy, Favras truly made his mark with one of the snarkiest last lines ever uttered. After reading his death warrant, Favras coolly stated:

"I see that you have made three spelling mistakes."

MARGARET SANGER (1879–1966)

Sanger's tireless efforts paved the way for legalized contraception and Planned Parenthood in the United States. She was a sex educator at a time when providing sex ed could land you in jail. She opened the first birth control clinic in the US in 1916 and spent much of her life communicating to the public across America, as well as in Japan, China, and Korea.

Despite a life of fighting the system, it seems that Sanger was able to keep a sense of humor right to the end. Her last words before finally succumbing to congestive heart failure at age eighty-six were:

"A party! Let's have a party."

KARL MARX (1818–1883)

Born in Prussia, died in London, and grew one heck of an amazing beard in the time in-between. He was also the father of communism and modern social science and one of the most influential thinkers of the last few hundred years.

Between his pamphlets, essays, articles, and other writings, including both *The Communist Manifesto* and *Das Kapital*,

Marx said a lot in his sixty-four years of life. His output was so prodigious in fact that, when asked on his deathbed if he had any last words, he responded:

"Go on, get out! Last words are for fools who haven't said enough."

SIR WALTER RALEIGH (1552–1618)

There are not a lot of people with the courage of Sir Walter Raleigh. Raleigh spent his life exploring and adventuring on behalf of queen and country. His more famous expeditions include Roanoke Island, Venezuela, and a quest to find the golden city of El Dorado. He also fought the Spanish Armada and was accused of plotting against James I. This last bit of business landed him in the Tower of London, where he turned his focus to writing.

Though the well-liked Raleigh was eventually pardoned, an unfortunate set of circumstances forced King James to reinstate his death sentence at the behest of an angry Spanish ambassador. In the end, Raleigh showed fealty to his king, refusing to escape his sentence and reportedly telling his executioner, "Let us dispatch. At this hour my ague comes upon me. I would not have my enemies think I quaked from fear." This resolve lasted right to the end, with Raleigh yelling:

"Strike, man, strike!"

ELEANOR ROOSEVELT (1884–1962)

First Lady from 1933 until the end of World War II in 1945, wife of President Franklin D. Roosevelt, and the woman Harry S. Truman once referred to as "First Lady of the world," Roosevelt was incredibly smart and liked by almost all around her from a young age. Outspoken, savagely funny, and quick as a whip, Roosevelt was active in the Civil Rights

Movement, the war effort, and more organizations and diplomatic efforts than can be listed here.

She died at age seventy-eight after events that began with her being hit by a car and ended with cardiac arrest brought on by tuberculosis. While she was on her deathbed, a nurse told her that she would die once the reason God put her on earth was fulfilled. Her response:

"Utter nonsense."

QUEEN VICTORIA (1819–1901)

Victoria reigned for sixty-three years. The Victorian era saw massive changes in the UK, an explosion of scientific discovery, and major changes in the realms of religion, industry, politics, economics, and migration.

Victoria was also madly in love with her husband, Prince Albert. The couple met in 1836 and corresponded by mail until their second meeting in 1838. It was apparently then that Victoria fell head over heels. She proposed five days later. She would write in her journal of the meeting and the proposal:

"I said to him that I thought he must be aware why I wished him to come here, and that it would make me too happy if he would consent to what I wished (to marry me); we embraced each other over and over again, and he was so kind, so affectionate; oh! To feel I was, and am, loved by such an angel as Albert."

When Albert died in 1861, Victoria fell into a deep depression. Her beloved husband remained foremost in her thoughts when she died forty years later. Her last word:

"Bertie."

THE ROMAN EMPIRE

The final words of the leaders of Rome are notoriously apocryphal. Some have been created for dramatic effect, others have been changed by the course of history, and some have simply been made up.

JULIUS CAESAR (100 BC–44 BC)

The last words we all know from Shakespeare's play have no historical basis. Sadly, the truth is much sadder than fiction. Rather than delivering the famous *"Et tu*, Brutus," it is believed that the real-life Caesar first called for help and then, in an act of submission, pulled his toga over his head and let Brutus finish him.

AUGUSTUS (63 BC–14 BC)

The first emperor of the Roman Empire has three sets of last words attributed to him, though there may be an explanation for this. His last words in public were "Behold, I found Rome of clay, and leave her to you of marble." His last famous words in private were "Have I played the part well? Then applaud as I exit." But apparently his actual final words were to his wife and were something along the lines of:

"Live mindful of our wedlock, Livia, and farewell."

CLAUDIUS (10 BC–54 AD)

Reports of his death are notoriously confused. He may or may not have been poisoned, and that poisoning may or may not have come at the hands of his wife Agrippina, and he may have died quickly or slowly, or recovered fully only to be poisoned again. Somewhere in the middle of all of this come some unfortunate last words that may or may not be related to a certain bodily function that might have been worsened by the possible poisoning:

"Oh dear, I've made a mess of it."

NERO (37 AD–68 AD)

Much like the story of Nero playing the fiddle while Rome burned around him, Nero's last words seem a bit too fitting to be true: "What an artist dies with me!"

HADRIAN (76 AD–138 AD)

Of all the emperors of Rome, it seems that Hadrian was the best prepared for death. Hadrian was known as something of a poet and, on his deathbed, he composed a short five-line poem. Unfortunately for Hadrian, even his best-laid plans

have gone awry as no two poets seem to be able to agree on
a correct translation of the poem, though most translations
tend to go something like this:

"Little soul, you charming little wanderer,

my body's guest and partner,

Where are you off to now?

Somewhere without color, savage and bare;

Never again to share a joke."

AMERICAN PRESIDENTS

Love them or hate them, the presidents of the United States of America have been the closest thing politics has had to rock stars for the past few centuries. That is not to say they were all memorable—for every Abraham Lincoln or Theodore Roosevelt there is a John Tyler or Benjamin Harrison—but even the duds were weird enough to be interesting.

Along with having quite a few interesting quirks, American presidents also have a remarkably good track record of having their last words saved for posterity. Some are heartwarming (Taylor), some are sad (Tyler), while many are reminders that, in the end we are all remarkably the same— some of us just get to die in a giant white mansion and have a bunch of streets and schools named after us.

In the interest of brevity, because so many presidents have had their last words recorded, here is a list of one interesting fact about each of the first thirty-seven presidents, along with their final words.

GEORGE WASHINGTON (1732–1799)

The one who was secretly a ginger.

Last Words: " 'Tis well."

JOHN ADAMS (1735–1826)

The one who thought the president should be referred to as "His Majesty."

Last Words: "Thomas Jefferson survives."

(Jefferson had actually died just a few hours earlier.)

THOMAS JEFFERSON (1743–1826)

The one who invented the swivel chair.

Last Words: "No, doctor, nothing more."

JAMES MADISON (1751–1836)

The one who had his White House burned down during a war with Canada.

Last Words: "I talk better lying down."

JAMES MONROE (1758–1831)

The third president to die on the Fourth of July.

Last Words: "I regret that I should leave this world without again beholding him."

(The him in question was his close friend James Madison.)

JOHN QUINCY ADAMS (1767–1848)

The one who started every day with a five o'clock in the morning skinny dip in the Potomac.

Last Words: "This is the last of earth. I am content."

ANDREW JACKSON (1767–1845)

The one who was involved in over a hundred duels.

Last Words: "I hope to meet each of you in heaven. Be good, children, all of you, and strive to be ready when the change comes."

MARTIN VAN BUREN (1782–1862)

The one who, kind of, invented the word "Okay."

Last Words: "There is but one reliance."

WILLIAM HENRY HARRISON (1773–1841)

The one who wouldn't wear a coat at his inauguration, caught a cold, and died thirty-three days later.

Last Words: "I wish you to understand the true principles of government. I wish them carried out. I ask nothing more."

(This was advice for Vice President John Tyler. Unfortunately, Harrison was delirious, and Tyler was not in the room, or the state.)

JOHN TYLER (1790–1862)

The one who fathered fifteen children.

Last Words: "Doctor, I am going... Perhaps it is best."

JAMES K. POLK (1795–1849)

The one who banned music and dancing from the White House.

Last Words: "I love you, Sarah. For all eternity, I love you."

ZACHARY TAYLOR (1784–1850)

The one nicknamed "old rough and ready" for his clothes and his willingness to fight.

Last Words: "I regret nothing, but I am sorry to leave my friends."

MILLARD FILLMORE (1800–1874)

The one who married his schoolteacher.
Last Words: "The nourishment is palatable."
(In reference to a bowl of soup.)

FRANKLIN PIERCE (1804–1869)

The one who was arrested for running over an old lady with a horse.

Last Words: Unknown.

JAMES BUCHANAN (1791–1868)

The unmarried one, whose niece acted as First Lady.

Last Words: "Oh, Lord God Almighty, as thou wilt!"

ABRAHAM LINCOLN (1809–1865)

The one who had a wrestling record of 299–1.

Last Words: "She won't think anything about it."

(In response to Mary Todd asking, "What will Miss Harris think of my hanging on to you so?" after he held her hand.)

ANDREW JOHNSON (1808–1875)

The one who escaped after being sold as a child to a tailor as an indentured apprentice.

Last Words: "Oh, do not cry. Be good children and we shall meet in heaven."

ULYSSES S. GRANT (1822–1885)

The one whose middle initial came from a West Point typo that stuck with him.

Last Word: "Water."

RUTHERFORD B. HAYES (1822–1893)

The one whose wife was the first First Lady to have a college degree.

Last Words: "I know I am going where Lucy is."

JAMES A. GARFIELD (1831–1881)

The ambidextrous one who could write Greek with one hand and Latin with the other, at the same time.

Last Words: "Oh, Swaim, can't you stop this?"

(Said to his doctor, who was trying to keep Garfield alive following a gunshot wound.)

CHESTER A. ARTHUR (1829–1886)

The one with the amazing sideburns.

Almost Last Words: "Life is not worth living."

(His last words are unknown, but these are close to his last.)

GROVER CLEVELAND (1837–1908)

The one who, at twenty-seven, bought his future wife her first stroller—she was a baby then.

Last Words: "I have tried so hard to do right."

BENJAMIN HARRISON (1833–1901)

The one who was terrified of electricity.

Last Words: "Are the doctors here? Doctor, my lungs..."

WILLIAM MCKINLEY (1843–1901)

The one who removed everything yellow from the White House because his wife hated yellow.

Last Words: "We are all going. We are all going. We are all going."

(In response to his wife who, watching him die of injuries from a gunshot wound, said: "I want to go too. I want to go too."

THEODORE ROOSEVELT (1858–1919)

The one who was shot in the chest before a speech but went on stage anyway, saying: "It takes more than that to kill a bull moose."

Last Words: "Put out the light."

(Said to an attendant before he went to bed.)

WILLIAM HOWARD TAFT (1857–1930)

The one who got stuck in a bathtub.

Last Words: Unknown.

WOODROW WILSON (1856–1924)

The one who had sheep that grazed on the White House lawn.

Last Words: "I am a broken piece of machinery. When the machinery is broken—I am ready."

WARREN G. HARDING (1865–1923)

The one who might have cheated on his wife in a White House closet.

Last Words: "That's good. Go on, read some more."

(Said to his wife, who was reading an article about him.)

CALVIN COOLIDGE (1872–1933)

The one who had a pygmy hippo named Billy.

Last Words: "Good morning, Robert." (Said to a carpenter just before Coolidge fell dead from a coronary thrombosis.)

HERBERT HOOVER (1874–1964)

The one who had two pet alligators.

Last Words: Unknown.

FRANKLIN D. ROOSEVELT (1882–1945)

The one who had a secret train line to take him from Grand Central to the basement of the Waldorf Astoria.

Last Words: "I have a terrific headache."

HARRY S. TRUMAN (1884–1972)

The one whose middle initial doesn't stand for anything.

Last Words: Unknown.

DWIGHT D. EISENHOWER (1890–1969)

The one who made more than 250 paintings.

Last Words: "I want to go. God take me."

JOHN F. KENNEDY (1917–1963)

The one who saved his shipwrecked crew by writing a message on a coconut.

Last Words: "No, you certainly can't."

(In response to Nellie Connally saying, "You can't say Dallas doesn't love you.")

LYNDON B. JOHNSON (1908–1973)

The one who had a Fresca fountain in the Oval Office.

Last Words: "Send Mike immediately."

RICHARD NIXON (1913–1994)

The one who had a bowling alley built in the White House basement.

His last word was: "Help."

CHAPTER FOUR

ATHLETES

Athletes live loud and fast. It is a profession built around shining brightly and briefly. There are few other jobs where you are over the hill at forty. The best of the best get a couple of decades in the limelight; most get much, much less.

In a way, though, it could be said that the greats live forever. Babe Ruth calling his shot, Wilt Chamberlain scoring one hundred points in a single game, Maradona punching the ball into the back of the net, the voice of the great Lou Gehrig echoing through the speakers at Yankee Stadium—these are moments that will withstand the test of time. As sportscasters love to say, these athletes are immortalized forever.

However, in another less metaphorical way, even the greats do actually die. Even if they have candy bars named after them and bronze statues and retired numbers, they still die. In fact, not only do they die, but they often die with bad knees. The aforementioned Babe Ruth is a great example of someone who used to be an athlete but is now a dead person. Some might say his 1927 Yankees were the greatest baseball team of all time, but even murderer's row can't out-murder the greatest murderer of all.

As Yogi Berra said, "It ain't over 'til it's over." And for the athletes listed below, it is in fact over.

YOGI BERRA (1925–2015)

Nobody has ever been more quotable than Yogi Berra. The New York Yankees catcher never met a phrase he couldn't turn. "When you come to a fork in the road, take it." "A nickel ain't worth a dime anymore." "It's like deja vu all over again." "The future ain't what it used to be." Berra's life was a tour de force of witticisms. So it is particularly unfortunate that his final words haven't been saved for posterity—though, in his later years, Yogi did leave us with this particularly insightful thought about death:

"Always go to other people's funerals, otherwise they won't go to yours."

PETE MARAVICH (1947–1988)

"Pistol" Pete was one of basketball's greats right from the start. Maravich holds the record for most points scored in a collegiate career with 3,667 for LSU. This record is even more amazing when you take into account that he accomplished it in only three years and before the introduction of the shot clock.

Once Pistol Pete got to the big leagues, the legend only grew with five all-star appearances and an NBA scoring title.

Sadly, Maravich's career was cut short due to injuries. Even more sadly, he had a defect in his heart, the symptoms of which had remained dormant until the moment of his death. His last words came during a pickup game, just seconds before his sudden heart attack:

"I feel great. I feel just great."

"Rowdy" Roddy Piper (1954–2015)

Piper was at the top of the list of wrestlers you loved to hate, and he would have it no other way. The Canadian who was billed from Glasgow, Scotland, had a quick right hand and an even quicker wit. He was Hulk Hogan's main foe at the original WrestleMania and would go on to be one of the most famous villains in wrestling history.

Nobody could deliver a promo like Piper—cool and collected one moment, laughing maniacally the next, flying off the handle into a wild rage, and then back to calm at a moment's notice. He could rile up a crowd to the edge of rioting in one city, and then get all twenty thousand fans chanting his name the following night. Even later in his career, as something of an antihero, Piper never lost his trademark temper or his caustic wit.

Piper would also go on to pursue a career in acting, the highlight of which was the lead role in John Carpenter's 1988 classic *They Live*. While we don't know the Rowdy One's last words, the final line of his last tweet could not be more fitting:

"YOU PICKED THE WRONG GUY TO BULLY!"

JOE DIMAGGIO (1914–1999)

The Yankee Clipper was one of the greatest who ever played the game of baseball. Joe was the heart and soul of one of the greatest Yankees teams of all time. He was a hard-hustling slugger with a terrific glove and a love of the game that couldn't be beat. Plus, he had the kind of warm smile and down-to-earth attitude that made him the epitome of the Average Joe. On the field, he could make his every dream come true; sadly, the same wasn't true for his love life outside the ballpark.

When it came to competing for the love of Marilyn Monroe, Joe wasn't just up against fellas that could swing the bat and run the bases; he was up against one of the greatest playwrights of all time and one of America's most beloved presidents. Monroe left Joe for Arthur Miller in 1955, and then rumors heavily suggest that she fell for JFK after that. DiMaggio never married again, and never got over his one true love. His last words:

"I'll finally get to see Marilyn."

MOE BERG (1902–1972)

Berg was known as the "Brainiest Guy in Baseball." While he never made a big splash in the major leagues, he was reportedly well-liked and spent over fifteen years between five teams in the big leagues, mostly as a backup catcher.

During World War II, Berg lived up to his brainy moniker as he became a spy for the US government, working undercover in Yugoslavia and in Italy, where he infiltrated a group of physicists to learn about Nazi nuclear projects.

Even after a life of espionage and intrigue, Berg never lost his love of baseball. His last words:

"How did the Mets do today?"

WALTER PAYTON (1954–1999)

It would be hard to find a football player more beloved by his peers than Walter Payton. Not only was Sweetness great on the field (nine Pro-Bowls, one Super Bowl, and way too many other things to name here), he was also great off the field.

His motto was "Never die easy," and he didn't. By the time Payton knew he had a rare liver disease, his window for a transplant had already passed, but that didn't stop him from using his last few months to tirelessly bring the need for organ transplants the national exposure it needed.

In his last days, author Don Yeager asked him if he felt like yelling at God. Payton responded:

"Are you serious? Something good is going to come of this. I just haven't figured out what it is yet."

ROBERTO CLEMENTE (1934–1972)

The first Latin American player ever to be inducted into the National Baseball Hall of Fame, Clemente was a hero right to the end. Clemente finished his pro career with exactly 3,000 hits and 240 home runs.

His career was cut short when, in 1972, Nicaragua was hit by a major earthquake. Clemente, who was known for his commitment to charity work, organized relief efforts and, after hearing that the first planes didn't make it to their destination, decided to get on the next plane and deliver the aid packages himself. Unfortunately, his plane was lost. Sadly, his last words were:

"If there is one more delay, we'll leave this for tomorrow."

MICKEY MANTLE (1931–1995)

One of the all-time Yankee greats, Mantle had a complicated relationship with both the fans and his friends. "The Mick" was known for being a gruff customer who had a problem with the bottle that hounded him for most of his life. His final days were a reflection of his late attempts to combat his demons. As he lay in a hospital bed at the end of a long fight with cancer, three of his old teammates came to visit. The last words he spoke were to them:

"You guys ain't leaving already, are you?"

Soon after, he slipped into unconsciousness, and his sons and his ex-wife Merlyn (who was the love of Mickey's life and the one person he really listened to) came to his bedside. Mickey's last sight was of her. As she squeezed his hand, he opened his eyes for just a moment before closing them again forever.

BABE RUTH (1895–1948)

In all of sports, there are few figures that loom as large as that of the Babe. His 714 career home runs are second only to Hank Aaron (for non-performance-enhanced players). The Bambino was such an amazing hitter that people forget he had two twenty-three-game winning seasons as a pitcher and won three World Series with the Red Sox, playing mostly on the mound. Those were famously Boston's last World Series wins for almost a century, due to the Curse of the Bambino that was put on the team when Babe was traded.

But it is in pinstripes that we all best remember the Sultan of Swat. For almost fifteen years, Babe *was* baseball. He was mythical—the called shot, the homer for Johnny Sylvester, the candy bar, the many, many, many late-night tales.

Sadly, the Yankee great was felled by a long bout with cancer that left him with just a shadow of his once impressive frame. On his last day, Babe was still up on his feet in his room. When a doctor asked him where he was off to, Babe answered:

"I'm going over the valley."

VINCE LOMBARDI (1913–1970)

Despite a common misconception, the Super Bowl is not the name of the trophy; it is the name of the game. The golden football that is handed out at the Super Bowl is actually the Lombardi Trophy, and it is named after one of the greatest coaches of all time.

Vince Lombardi coached the Green Bay Packers from 1959 to 1967, winning NFL Coach of the Year in his first season, a conference title in his second, and a Super Bowl in his third. His teams would go on to win a total of five Super Bowls in seven years. He was also known as a stalwart for civil rights, leading the Packers to be the first NFL team that was integrated on and off the field.

Like many great figures in the world of sports, Lombardi
was not an easy man to live with—though by all accounts
he met his match in Marie Planitz, whose quick wit and
strong character were more than up to the task. When Coach
Lombardi died of cancer in 1970, his last words were to her:

"Happy Anniversary. I love you."

CHAPTER FIVE

LAST WORDS IN FILM

In real life, we only get one crack at last lines, and honestly, most of us are a bit too preoccupied with dying to make the most of the moment. But wouldn't it be great if we had multiple takes, a team of writers, and a director?

Let's take a pause from actual life-and-death—mostly death—situations, and instead look at some of the most memorable last words ever captured on film. And in true show-business fashion, let's do it in a classic top-ten countdown.

Spoiler Warning: This section contains the last words of characters from famous movies, which means that those characters die. You probably already know that all of them die because all of these movies are classics, and you have either seen them or heard them referenced enough times to feel like you have seen them. Although—let's be honest—if you haven't seen *Star Wars* or *Lord of The Rings* or *Terminator 2* by now, you have lost your chance to complain about spoilers, unless you are under twelve, and in that case, why are you reading this book about death and last words? Go find a Choose Your Own Adventure book or, better yet, go and watch *Star Wars*. Don't worry, nobody dies in it, so you can feel free to get really attached to them all, especially any kindly old men who live in the desert.

10. ROCKY IV (1985)

If you are thirteen, having a sleepover, and want to watch a Rocky movie, this is the one you should watch. This film sets an unbreakable record for montages per minute, plus it has one of the weirdest talking robots in movie history.

This is the one where Rocky ends the Cold War by getting punched a lot and not falling over. It comes right after the one where Rocky and Apollo become best friends and hop about in the ocean together in slow motion.

In *Rocky III*, Apollo finishes the film with one last fight, which follows his retirement fight in *Rocky II* and his "There ain't gonna be no rematch" fight in the original *Rocky*, so it is not surprising that *Rocky IV* begins with Apollo having his last, last, last fight. It's a fight that begins with the greatest, James Brown-iest entrance that has ever happened, either on film or in real life, and ends with the death of a character we spent four films learning to love. Sadly, like every movie cop on their last day before retirement, Apollo doesn't see the hand of fate reaching for him and, even though he is getting pummeled by the flat-topped pride of the USSR, he tells Rocky not to throw in the towel. The ensuing line is foreshadowing at its saddest.

Apollo's last words:

"I want you to promise me you're not gonna stop this fight, no matter what. No matter what!"

9. TITANIC (1997)

A good rule in life is if someone says that a car is uncrashable or a fortress is impenetrable or a boat is unsinkable, do not go near it. Whatever the thing is that can't happen will definitely, 100 percent happen.

This was of course the case with the Titanic, but unfortunately Jack, Rose, and Billy Zane didn't heed the above advice. Worse yet for Jack, he fell in love with a lady who needed a whole floating door all to herself.

All kidding aside, who among us didn't cry when Jack slowly sank into the icy waters of the Atlantic?

Jack's last words:

"Promise me, Rose. And never let go of that promise."

8. SCARFACE (1983)

The favorite movie of gangsters everywhere, *Scarface* has become a kind of cultural phenomenon—which is an amazing feat, considering it has a three-minute-long montage set to "Push It to the Limit" where Tony gets married, helps his wife find a new dress, and shows his friends a tiger. That said, it does have a high body count and approximately 182 F-words (which apparently is the reason for the number in Blink-182's name).

Al Pacino's Tony Montana is one of the most memorable characters in film history. At least one in every three people over thirty does an impression of him, and a quarter of those aren't bad. Just about everything Tony says is quote-worthy. Who among us hasn't been guilty of using "Say hello to my little friend" at some point in their life? Tony's last lines are no different, as he stands and taunts his attackers even as he is getting mowed down by a wave of bullets:

Tony's last words:

"Go ahead! I take your f—ing bullets! You think you kill me with bullets? I take your f—ing bullets! Go ahead!"

7. BRAVEHEART (1995)

Mel Gibson's famously loose retelling of the story of William Wallace is not without its faults. In fact, it is pretty darn packed with them. Instead of listing all the inaccuracies, let's just say that if *Braveheart* were an essay for a history class, it would be hard pressed to get a passing grade.

It does, however, have plenty of face-painting and sword-clashing and underdog rebellions and a lot of other things that folks go to the movies for. All of which was enough to even secure the film a somewhat surprising Best Picture nod at the sixty-eighth Academy Awards.

For better or worse, the film also has Gibson himself, broken Scottish accent and all, yelling his way through a plethora of quotable lines. Although none is more easily quotable than his final rebellious cry, just before his notably painful death:

William's last words:

"Freeeeeeeeedom!"

6. BUTCH CASSIDY AND THE SUNDANCE KID (1969)

There are very few duos in the history of Westerns that are more fun to watch than Butch and Sundance. Paul Newman and Robert Redford's real-life friendship is evident on screen, and it is an absolute blast to watch. It was almost too many blue eyes and too much smooth nonchalance for one film to handle.

While it would be entertaining to watch Newman and Redford do just about anything, it is an absolute delight watching them in a well-crafted film, loosely based on two of the Wild West's greatest outlaws on the run from lawman Joe Lefors. The film goes from train robberies to daring cliff-jumping escapes to what is maybe the best freeze-frame finale of all time. As Butch and Sundance are pinned down with no hope of escape, they manage a final quick bit of banter before going out with guns a-blazing:

Butch: "Wait a minute—you didn't see Lefors out there, did you?"

Sundance: "Lefors? No, why?"

Butch: "Oh, good. For a moment there, I thought we were in trouble."

5. STAR WARS (1977)

There is no film series more loved than Star Wars. Remember the first time you saw it? The epic crawl, Darth Vader's amazing music, Luke standing on the ridge looking at the binary sunset, Porkins vibrating like crazy before he explodes. It was the absolute best. And no amount of added scenes with Jabba having his tail stepped on or Greedo shooting first can change that.

Right at the center of all of that epic coolness was one incredibly chill old man. Every time Obi-Wan speaks, we listen. He doesn't need to raise his voice or get excited (unless he is chasing off Tusken Raiders). Old Ben is so laid-back he may as well be napping. Remember when he cut that one guy's arm off in the cantina and then ordered a drink like nothing happened? How cool was that?

When we do finally get to Obi-Wan's big confrontation with the one guy in the universe who might be able to rile him up, not only does he not get riled, he actually manages to make himself even more chill. So chill in fact that he literally calms himself to the point where he disappears and becomes a force ghost.

Obi-Wan's last words as a non-ghost:

"You can't win, Darth. If you strike me down, I shall become more powerful than you could possibly imagine."

4. LORD OF THE RINGS: THE FELLOWSHIP OF THE RING (2001)

There is an internet meme going around about how Sean Bean dies in everything he is in. But in actual fact, the only things he has died in are *Caravaggio*, *War Requiem*, *The Field*, *Lorna Doone*, *Tell Me That You Love Me*, *Scarlett*, *Clarissa*, *Patriot Games*, *GoldenEye*, *Don't Say a Word*, *Henry VIII*, *The Island*, *Far North*, *Black Death*, *Game of Thrones*, *Airborne*, *Red Riding*, *Essex Boys*, *Equilibrium*, *Cash*, *The Hitcher*, *Outlaw*, *Death Race 2*, *Age of Heroes*, and *Lord of the Rings: The Fellowship of the Ring*.

Out of that list of twenty-five on-screen deaths, which include stabbing, hanging, exploding, burying, death by stampede, and nine separate shootings, the one that stands out above them all is the belly full of arrows he takes as Boromir in the first film of the Lord of the Rings trilogy.

No matter what Boromir almost did or what drove him to it, his last seconds of redemption are some of the best moments in one of the best films of one of the best series of all time.

Boromir's last words:

"I would have followed you, my brother...my captain... my king."

3. 2001: A Space Odyssey (1968)

To say that *2001* was ahead of its time is the understatement of all understatements. Kubrick filmed what a moon landing would look like, a year before there had even been a moon landing. He did it so well, he inspired a conspiracy theory that thrives to this day. What is even more impressive is that the moon landing is just a tiny part of a film that hits an eerie number of nails right on the head.

Based on the book by Arthur C. Clarke, Kubrick's film set the bar for every sci-fi film that would follow. The film is well-researched, expertly shot, and stylistically breathtaking. You can almost pick out the exact shots that inspired films like *Star Wars*, *Interstellar*, *Gravity*, and hundreds of others. But at the heart of it all is one heck of a memorable villain.

Visually, HAL 9000 is just a bunch of red dots on a series of wall panels, a disembodied voice programmed to be soft, reassuring, and infinitely agreeable. As HAL reminds us, a 9000 model has never made a mistake. In the real world, this would be a selling point, but in the world of film, it is a foreshadowing of impending doom. Much like the Alexa you have in your living room and the Siri on your phone, HAL hears everything, sees everything, and controls everything, which is not ideal when things go awry.

Though HAL does inevitably turn on the humans it was built to protect, Kubrick manages to breathe a humanity into the AI that makes for a heartbreaking "death." As Dave slowly disconnects one circuit after another, HAL tries desperately to hold onto its sanity before finally fading away, singing the song it learned when it became operational in Urbana, Illinois, on the 12th of January, 1992.

HAL 9000's last words:

"Daisy, Daisy, give me your answer do. I'm half-crazy all for the love of you. It won't be a stylish marriage; I can't afford a carriage. But you'll look sweet upon the seat of a bicycle built for two."

2. CITIZEN KANE (1941)

If you look at any list of the greatest films of all time, you are all but guaranteed to find this one right at the top. Orson Welles's first feature film is also his masterpiece. The film is the directorial equivalent of someone not knowing that things are impossible and doing them anyway. It would be groundbreaking today; in 1941 it practically shattered the earth, even if it did get passed over for Best Picture in favor of *How Green Was My Valley*.

The film centers around a last word. It is the first word in the movie, the last word out of the mouth of its titular character, the white rabbit that leads newspaperman Jerry Thompson on his journey of discovery, and the final word read on the side of an old discarded sled before the screen fades to black.

Charles Foster Kane's last word:

"Rosebud."

1. THE WIZARD OF OZ (1939)

The Wizard of Oz is rightfully regarded as one of the greatest films ever made; the L. Frank Baum book series it is based on is also wonderful. However, one must question giving a supposedly all-powerful character a weakness that is basically everywhere all the time.

The Wicked Witch of the West would have had to avoid baths, showers, rain, snow, sweat, Snapple, and soups of all kinds. The list goes on and on. For a big bad witch, this was a pretty severe and unfortunate allergy.

In the book, the Wicked Witch actually plays a fairly small part, but, once you see Margaret Hamilton's phenomenal performance, it is easy to see why the character wasn't just expanded for the film, but eventually went on to inspire a hugely successful Broadway musical.

The Wicked Witch's last words:

"I'm melting! Melting! Oh, what a world! What a world! Who ever thought a little girl like you could destroy my beautiful wickedness?! Ah, I'm going! Ahhh!"

CHAPTER SIX

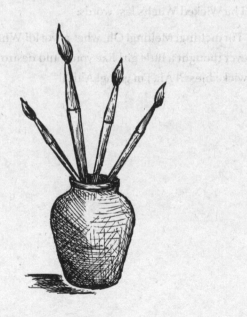

ARTISTS

While they may be known more for their pictures than their words, it isn't a surprise that beautiful minds are capable of saying beautiful things. Artists reframe the way we see the world; they show us the mundane through a new set of eyes and manipulate form, color, and shape into keys that unlock new sensations. These are people who see the truth that lies beneath the dust or behind the shiny facade. Many great artists wear their hearts on their canvases, giving any perceptive onlooker a window to the soul. At least some of them do. Others paint really nice bowls of fruit that look great on office walls.

The other thing artists are particularly well-known for is being better appreciated after their deaths, which makes this a perfect time to appreciate these men and women.

SALVADOR DALI (1904–1999)

The Spanish surrealist is known for his work featuring super-long-legged elephants and melting clocks. Though he is almost as well-known for his larger-than-life personality. Dali famously said things like "I don't do drugs. I am drugs," and "Each morning when I awake, I experience again a supreme pleasure—that of being Salvador Dali."

With his gravity-defying moustache, his overt eccentricities, and his interest in all things strange, Dali's life in many ways mimicked the strange worlds he depicted. With his last words, Dali took another opportunity for life to imitate art:

"Where is my clock?"

LEONARDO DA VINCI (1452-1519)

Da Vinci believed that art and science worked hand in hand, and, judging by his mastery of both, it seems that he might be right. It would take a book twice as long as this one to even start to describe his life and work.

He painted two of the world's best-known pieces of art: the *Mona Lisa* and *The Last Supper*. He drafted blueprints for bridges, flying machines, crossbows, and parachutes. He created a functioning robotic knight and invented scuba gear. He improved the clock. His sketches of human anatomy and understanding of what would later be known as biomechanics were centuries ahead of his contemporaries. And, even after all of that, he still wasn't satisfied with what he had accomplished.

His last words:

"I have offended God and mankind because my work did not reach the quality it should have."

RAPHAEL (1483–1520)

Despite what the stories of cartoon turtles would have you believe, the real-life Raphael, Michelangelo, and Leonardo were actually rivals. Donatello died in 1466, so he was already sixty-four when da Vinci was born, and he was dead and gone about ten years before the birth of Michelangelo and almost two decades before Raphael was born.

Of these four great Renaissance masters, Raphael was the youngest and died the earliest (at only thirty-seven). Though his time in the sun was short, he was incredibly prolific. He left the world with hundreds of paintings, frescoes, and prints, along with his many architectural works.

Unlike his hotheaded amphibious counterpart, the painter was known for being particularly level-headed and was often called on to quell arguments. Later in his short career, he ran a workshop of more than fifty pupils which was famous for its harmonious sense of collaboration.

His last word:

"Happy."

FRIDA KAHLO (1907–1954)

Kahlo is best known for her self-portraits, but those are just part of her impressive body of work and even more impressive life. Much of Kahlo's work is inspired by the magical realism that permeates much of South and Central American art and culture.

Like many of the greats, her art was about more than beauty. She was a strong feminist, heavily involved in politics, and proud of her Mexican heritage. Many admire her non-idealized depictions of beauty and the female form.

Her last words capture the same unique blend that has made her art so important. They are equal parts beautiful, sensible, honest, and haunting:

"I hope the exit is joyful and hope never to return."

VINCENT VAN GOGH (1853–1890)

Van Gogh is the ultimate example of a great artist who was not appreciated in his own time. Today many of his works, including *Sunflowers*, *Bedroom in Aries*, and *The Starry Night*, have become household names. Sadly, none of this success was realized during his short thirty-seven years of life.

The Dutch painter spent many of his years living in poverty and famously battled with both alcoholism and mental illness throughout his lifetime. He is seen by many as the epitome of the starving artist. Van Gogh was singularly dedicated to his work and often used his paintings to express his true inner feelings, which sadly were often of isolation and despair.

One need only look at one of van Gogh's famous self-portraits to see both the struggles that lie within and the extraordinary bittersweet beauty that the great artist was capable of.

Sadly, van Gogh died after walking to the hospital following a self-inflicted gunshot wound.

His last words:

"The sadness will last forever."

PABLO PICASSO (1881–1973)

On the opposite end of the spectrum from van Gogh is Pablo Picasso. Picasso was an artist who was widely renowned as a genius during his lifetime and who managed to amass a fortune during his long and prolific career.

If you asked someone on the street to name an artist, Picasso is most likely the name you would get. Even the most casual fans of art are likely to have some knowledge of works such as *The Old Guitarist*, *Seated Woman*, and *La Rêve*. While Picasso worked in a number of styles, he is best known for his work with Cubism, which attempted to bring a third dimension to a two-dimensional medium by breaking subjects into pieces and then looking at those pieces from different viewpoints at the same time.

Picasso died at ninety-one from a heart attack while he and his wife were having dinner with friends. His last words:

"Drink to me, drink to my health, you know I can't drink anymore."

HENRI DE TOULOUSE-LAUTREC (1864–1901)

Toulouse-Lautrec was the artist of record for the world-famous Montmartre scene in Paris, where he drank and smoked and ate (and did a lot of other things) with a cadre of colorful philosophers, writers, actors, artists, dancers, prostitutes, and comedians.

Much of his work centers around his life in Montmartre, the nightlife at the Moulin Rouge and other such haunts, and the people that made up the bohemian community that he was part of. He has been colorfully portrayed in films including *Moulin Rouge* and *Midnight in Paris*.

He is also well-known for his short stature, growing to only four foot eight. In his mid-teens, he broke both of his legs, and, as the result of a rare genetic disorder, now known as Toulouse-Lautrec Syndrome, his legs ceased growing while the rest of his body continued. (It has been heavily rumored that another "area" below his belt was actually hypertrophied, which means that unlike his legs it did in fact continue to grow, and then some.)

Toulouse-Lautrec died at only thirty-six from complications caused by a combination of alcoholism and syphilis. His last words were directed at his father, whom he did not see often and was not close with:

"Vieux con!"

("Old fart!")

PAUL CÉZANNE (1839–1906)

Cézanne is best known for his work with still life, including a number of paintings of apples. Though he did produce several well-known works in a wide range of styles, much of the French artist's work was driven by a desire to capture nature in an authentic manner.

He had strong convictions about the purpose of art and often spoke and wrote about the subject, famously saying things like: "An art which isn't based on feeling isn't an art at all," "Painting from nature is not copying the object; it is realizing one's sensations," and "Genius is the ability to renew one's emotions in daily experience."

Though Cézanne's work now hangs in almost every major gallery worth mentioning, during his life he had difficulty being taken seriously. Early in Cézanne's career, a curator named Pontier somewhat famously refused to show his work. This snub in particular obviously stayed with the painter throughout his career, as it is suggested that Cézanne's last word was:

"Pontier."

GUSTAV KLIMT (1862–1918)

There is an episode in the fourth season of *Buffy the Vampire Slayer* in which vampires who live under a university are keeping a running tally of which posters they find on the dorm room walls of their victims: Klimt's *The Kiss* or Monet's *Waterlilies*. It's funny because it's so true; Klimt prints are as much a part of a twenty-year-old's first decor as Ikea coffee tables and milk-crate bookshelves.

There is a quality to Klimt's work, which is largely influenced by Japanese style and methods, that is relatable, sensual, and obviously beautiful, even if it is deceptively complex. The irony of his popularity is that, during his life, much of his work was seen as overly erotic, and in some cases was even deemed pornographic. Klimt's focus on sex reportedly transcended the canvas, as he is rumored to have sired fourteen illegitimate children with a number of women.

Perhaps most interesting of all Klimt's relationships was the one he had with a woman named Emilie, whom he remained close with for decades but is said to have never been physically romantic with. When Klimt died, she was in the forefront of his thoughts.

His last words:

"Get Emilie."

BERTHE MORISOT (1841–1895)

One of the more important impressionist painters, Morisot captured the essence of everyday life with light and color. Morisot was successful in her lifetime and enjoyed close friendships and the support of many greats of the time including Renoir, Degas, Cézanne, and Monet. She was also married to Eugene Manet, brother of famed artist Edouard.

Morisot was a prolific artist, creating hundreds of pieces over her life. She often focused on slice-of-life scenes of women and children, often using her daughter and her sister as her subjects.

Morisot died at only fifty-three, becoming ill while tending to her daughter, who had contracted influenza. Leaving Julie an orphan at only sixteen, Morisot wrote a letter to her daughter on her deathbed. While we don't know Morisot's final words, we do know that in the letter she wrote:

"You never caused me pain in your little life... You have looks and money. Use them well."

CHAPTER SEVEN

MUSICIANS

Sadly, of all the categories of celebrities, the ones that are most famous for dying are musicians. Perhaps it is fitting that so many musician deaths rock the world. They make their living spilling their guts to the world, standing live on stage in front of millions and laying out their souls night after night. It only makes sense that, when they die, the world hears about it. Many of these deaths come tragically young. Some come as a result of the rock 'n' roll lifestyle, others as a by-product of the same soul-baring openness and fragile genius that skyrocketed many of these stars to fame and fortune.

It is ironic that so many of these stars had their deaths immortalized in song: "American Pie," "Real Good Looking Boy," "Angel of Harlem," and Puff Daddy and Faith Hill's classic "I'll Be Missing You." If music is the soundtrack of life, these singers, guitar players, and composers all left the world with one last memorable note.

BOB MARLEY (1945–1981)

The Jamaican-born singer, songwriter, and revolutionary brought the sounds of his country to the world. Both with his band the Wailers and later as a solo artist, Marley took the sounds of reggae, ska, rock, and folk and created something both universal and distinct.

When you think about the amazing catalogue of hits he created and the impact he left on the world, it is easy to forget how young he was when he died. And he didn't just leave us with hits; he left us with songs that are beloved by the world all over. "No Woman No Cry," "Three Little Birds," "Redemption Song," "Is This Love," "Jamming," "Buffalo Soldier," "One Love"—the list goes on and on. These are songs that inspired love and peace but also helped spark revolution and reminded us not to stand for injustice.

His last words were to his son Ziggy and encapsulate so much that set the musician apart:

"Money can't buy life."

GEORGE HARRISON (1943–2001)

You can tell a lot about a person by their favorite Beatle—especially if that Beatle is George Harrison. George was the shy one, the enigma, the sensitive one with a bit of an edge. He played slightly off-kilter songs on slightly off-kilter instruments. Also, he could really play guitar.

As much as John and Paul were the face of the band and the ones with their names on the hits, George was always just in the background, pushing the group musically and spiritually to break new ground. Without George in the fold, it is doubtful that there would have been a *Revolver*, or a *Sgt. Pepper's Lonely Hearts Club Band*, or a *White Album*.

Much of his music focused on finding peace both within
and without, so it is only fitting that, as he passed away from
cancer with his wife by his side, his final words were ones
of love.

His last words:

"Love one another."

AMY WINEHOUSE (1983–2011)

Amy Winehouse only released two albums in her tragically
short life. But even with that small sample size, it is clear that
she was something special. The so-cool-it-hurts timelessness
of "Back to Black," the blend of punk sensibility and
throwback composition of "Rehab." If these were the seeds,
just imagine what was to come. Sadly, "Rehab" wasn't just
her biggest hit; it was also a bit of dark foreshadowing of the
sad fate to come.

Unfortunately, Winehouse dealt with a number of both private and not-so-private demons, including well-documented drug and alcohol abuse, mental illness, and a number of run-ins with the law. Sadly, her vices caught up to her, ending her life at only twenty-seven years old. Sadder still are reports that she had visited her GP just hours before her death and had told her doctor:

"I don't want to die."

LUDWIG VAN BEETHOVEN (1770–1827)

There is a short list of composers who have soundtracked the modern world: Tchaikovsky, Mozart, Brahms, Bach, but right near the top of that list is the Swiss-born composer who once time-traveled with Bill and Ted. "Für Elise" and the Fifth and Ninth Symphonies have become part of the collective consciousness.

It is well-known that Beethoven wrote many of his greatest works after losing his hearing, but what many don't know is that the composer didn't lose his hearing until he was twenty-eight, and the exact scope and cause of his hearing loss is a matter of some debate. One interesting, if debatable, theory is that it may have been at least in part due to his habit of dunking his head into bowls of freezing water in order to stay awake.

There is also some controversy about his last words. Some have suggested that they were "Applaud, my friends, the comedy is finished." Others claim that they were the somewhat ironic "I shall hear in heaven." Perhaps the most accepted account is that his final words came just after he was told that wine was on its way to his deathbed:

"Pity, pity, too late."

WOLFGANG AMADEUS MOZART (1756–1791)

He started writing music when he was four, started touring when he was six, completed his first symphony at eight, and, at fourteen, wrote an opera. Mozart made the most of his thirty-five years, composing more than six hundred works, including many of the world's best known and loved symphonies, concertos, and operas.

Mozart lived a lot in his short life. He traveled, he fell in love, he butted heads with an archbishop, he finally convinced the woman he loved to marry him (the day before a letter arrived from her father granting permission), he made a lot of money, and he spent a lot of money. One aspect of his life that has been overblown is his famous feud with fellow composer Antonio Salieri. While Mozart and Salieri may have been rivals at one point, there is evidence that in later life they were collegial and perhaps even friends; however, rumors persisted throughout Salieri's lifetime that he had poisoned his one-time rival. These rumors eventually led to Salieri's poor mental health in later life.

Mozart's cause of death remains a mystery, with theories invoking all nature of illness to less grounded suggestions of foul play at the hands of rivals, or even his own wife. Whatever the cause, Mozart knew when the end had come.

His last words:

"The taste of death is upon my lips. I feel something that is not of this earth."

Kurt Cobain (1967–1994)

Anyone who grew up in the 1990s remembers the first time they heard the distinctive opening riff of "Smells Like Teen Spirit." It was a spark that set off an explosion in the music industry. The song perfectly distills both a nascent Seattle music scene and the turmoil bubbling under the surface of just about every sixteen-year-old in the world. And it was perhaps not even the album's best song.

Nirvana's growth over the course of their three albums, released between 1989 and 1994, was astronomical. All three albums are classics, but the trajectory from messy garage rock to sonic art hinted at amazing things to come. Cobain was, of course, the driving force behind the band's soul-baring lyrics, sucking in listeners with vocals that could swing from delicate to primal in an instant. Sadly, the demons that Cobain seemed to be attempting to exorcise in his music were all too real. The singer took his own life at only twenty-seven years of age, leaving these as his last words:

"I don't have the passion anymore, and so remember, it's better to burn out than to fade away. Peace, love, empathy."

Frank Sinatra (1915–1998)

There are very few performers who could command a room like Ol' Blue Eyes. The leader of the Rat Pack (a phrase which Frank himself was not fond of) did a bit of everything, and he did it well. Sinatra has sold more than 150 million albums worldwide, earned an Academy Award for his acting, and is often credited with helping skyrocket the popularity of Las Vegas.

At the heart of Sinatra's success is his ability to make any song his own. Close your eyes and think of the tune to "My Way," or "The Lady Is a Tramp." Did you hear it in Sinatra's voice? Of course you did. He didn't always sing it first or even best, but once Frank put his stamp on a song, it was his.

Though he had a rapier wit and a silver tongue, the Chairman of the Board was also tough as nails. Right up until his death at eighty-two, Sinatra was known as a man who got what he wanted how he wanted it. While his last words could be taken as an admission of defeat, it is just as likely that they were somewhere between blunt honesty and dark wit. On his deathbed, his wife encouraged him to fight. His reply:

"I'm losing."

GLENN MILLER (1904–1944)

While a lot of people have been given the nickname over the years, it is hard to argue that Glenn Miller isn't the true King of Swing. At his peak, leading up to his untimely death, Miller managed a mind-boggling sixteen number-one hits and sixty-nine top tens in just four years. Between 1939 and 1943, he was the best-selling musician in the world, with timeless hits like "Little Brown Jug," "Chattanooga Choo-Choo," and "Pennsylvania 6-500."

The only thing that slowed down Miller's success was his desire to do his part for the armed forces in World War

II. While Miller was too old to be drafted into service, he
pledged to help the troops the best way he knew how and
became the leader of the Army Air Forces Band. Sadly, this
decision would lead to his early death. In December of 1944,
Glenn Miller boarded a flight set to take him from London
to the troops serving in Paris. His flight was lost over the
English Channel.

The legend is that his last words as he boarded the plane in
London were:

"Where the hell are the parachutes?"

ELVIS PRESLEY (1935–1977)

Elvis once famously said, "The image is one thing and the
human being is another. It's very hard to live up to an image,
put it that way." Nobody had a larger image to live up to than
Elvis. The best-selling recording artist in the history of music

became such an icon that he was known simply as the King. If you have heard of music, you have heard of Elvis.

It has been reported that Graceland still receives somewhere between 500,000 and 750,000 visitors a year. The only house in America that outstrips those numbers is the White House.

While the specifics of his cause of death are disputed, Elvis died of a heart attack at the age of forty-two, likely due to some combination of an enlarged heart and the use of both prescription and non-prescription drugs. According to his former fiancée Ginger Alden, his final words were:

"I'm going to the bathroom to read."

SAM COOKE (1931–1964)

There are far too many on this list of musicians who died far too early, but it would be hard to find a more tragic loss to the world than Sam Cooke. At the height of his popularity during the Civil Rights Movement of the late 1950s and early '60s, Cooke was on the front line, breaking down color barriers both on and off the airwaves.

What might be most incredible about Cooke's huge popularity is that he was such a tremendous musician; he managed to not only score hits with catchy pop songs and heart-melting ballads like "Another Saturday Night" and "You Send Me," he also got mainstream radio to play overtly political tracks such as "A Change Is Gonna Come" and "Chain Gang." Whether it was Gospel versus secular, rock 'n' roll versus R&B, and most importantly black versus white, there wasn't a wall in music that Cooke wasn't breaking down.

Sadly, the brave leader with a voice as smooth as silk was gunned down at his hotel at the age of thirty-three. His last words:

"Lady, you shot me."

BUDDY RICH (1917–1987)

There has perhaps never been a drummer as influential as Buddy Rich. A child prodigy who grew into a legend, Rich was the backbone of bands led by such giants as Tommy Dorsey and Count Basie. He was known for being fast, versatile, and explosive, but unfortunately this was true both on stage and off. Rich's temper was almost as famous as his virtuoso playing.

Buddy's outbursts became so famous that band members began recording them. It seems that Rich had a sense of humor about the whole thing, as on his deathbed he asked close friend and biographer Mel Tormé to play one of the recordings for him, though apparently Tormé never did.

Rich was a larger-than-life figure, and with that came some larger-than-life stories. An oft-disputed story is that of his final words. The legend goes that a nurse asked Buddy if there was anything he couldn't take. Rich replied:

"Yeah, country music!"

EDITH PIAF (1915–1963)

The French singer was given her adopted last name (which is French for sparrow) for her memorable voice, and memorable it was. Piaf is one of the great torch singers, perhaps most famous for her classic song "La Vie en Rose."

Piaf lived a most remarkable life. She was raised in a brothel run by her grandmother and performed acrobatics with her street-performer father. She had ties to the mafia, the love of her life died in a plane crash, she appeared in a film by Jean Cocteau, she helped prisoners escape from German camps during World War II, and all of that is just the tip of the iceberg.

In the end, she was felled by a combination of alcohol abuse and substance addiction. Her last words were:

"Every damn thing you do in this life, you have to pay for."

FREDDIE MERCURY (1946–1991)

The front man of Queen was known for his remarkable vocal range and incredible showmanship. It is rumored that Mercury had a four-octave range (for those not well-versed in singing, that is a very impressive feat). But even with his range, what may have been the most impressive aspect of Mercury's prowess as a singer was his versatility. Listen to any best of Queen collection and you will hear hints of disco, country, prog rock, opera, blues, jazz, hard rock, and pretty much any other genre you can think of.

As well-known as Mercury was for his voice and his stagemanship, he is equally famous for his personal life. Mercury was one of the first openly gay music stars and was known for living with as much gusto offstage as he did on it, sometimes to the detriment of his other relationships. It also cannot be overstated just how much he loved cats.

While there isn't certainty about Mercury's last words, it has been reported that he died at his home in the arms of his love, Jim Hutton. What is known are the final words of his last recorded interview:

"I still love you."

HUDDIE "LEAD BELLY" LEDBETTER (1888-1949)

While there is some disagreement about the spelling of his nickname, it is unanimously agreed that Lead Belly (or Leadbelly) could play the lights out. The virtuoso twelve-string guitar player could play pretty much anything you put in front of him. Mandolin, piano, violin, accordion, harmonica—he played them all. Plus, he could really write a song. His music has been covered by everyone who is anyone: Elvis Presley, Johnny Cash, the Beach Boys, White Stripes, Nirvana, Ministry, Led Zeppelin, Tom Waits, ABBA, Bob Dylan, Raffi, Red Hot Chili Peppers, Frank Sinatra, and the list goes on and on across genres and generations.

The gospel and blues man led a tumultuous life. Convicted several times in stabbing incidents, Lead Belly spent several years serving various prison sentences. He wouldn't come to fame until he moved to New York in later life and shortly afterward would be diagnosed with ALS.

He died at sixty-one. Reportedly his last, or near last, words were directed at his doctor:

"Doctor, if I put this here guitar down now, I ain't never gonna wake up."

JACKIE WILSON (1934–1984)

Mr. Excitement got his nickname by being one of the most engaging performers of his time. On top of Wilson's highly energetic stage presence, he also had a smooth and versatile voice that scored him over fifty hits in a range of genres including pop, R&B, and gospel.

To give his energetic shows a bit of extra oomph, Wilson reportedly had a habit of eating salt tablets and drinking large amounts of water before he hit the stage. The purpose behind his strange habit was to increase sweating. This likely led to hypertension and, in turn, to the massive heart attack that hit the singer during a performance on Dick Clark's Good Ol' Rock and Roll Revue. The heart attack left Wilson in a coma that lasted more than eight years until his death in 1984.

Wilson was unable to speak after the heart attack, which meant his final words came while doing what he lived for, performing to a room full of adoring fans. His heart attack happened while he was singing his hit song "Lonely Teardrops." His last line:

"My heart is crying, crying."

JEAN-PHILIPPE RAMEAU (1683-1764)

Much of Rameau's life is a mystery, but we do know he was a late bloomer. The French composer didn't make any sort of mark on the music world until his forties and didn't compose his first opera until he was almost fifty. Once he got rolling, he really got rolling, composing almost thirty pieces before his death.

Rameau was single-minded about his music. Not much of a conversationalist, and quick of temper, Rameau's musical talent and perfectionism got him through the door. His commitment to the art of music came into play on his deathbed. While Rameau lay ill with fever, a priest at his bedside tried to ease his pain with a song, which sparked the Frenchman's final words:

"What the devil do you mean to sing to me, priest? You are out of tune."

JOHNNY ACE (1929–1954)

You may have never heard the name Johnny Ace, but odds are that you have heard his music. His posthumous hit "Pledging My Love" plays in Lorraine's car in *Back to the Future,* as well as in both John Carpenter's *Christine* and Martin Scorsese's *Mean Streets*. It was also covered by Elvis Presley in the King's final studio session. Paul Simon even penned a touching song about him called "The Late Great Johnny Ace."

Sadly, the young singer's life was cut short right at the beginning of his budding career. The story goes that Johnny was backstage between sets and was playing with a gun in the dressing room. When others in the room asked him to put it away, he instead pointed the gun at his head.

Apparently, he thought there wasn't a bullet in the barrel, so, with a smile on his face, he pulled the trigger. His last words:

"It's okay! Gun's not loaded...see?"

TERRY KATH (1946–1978)

Kath played guitar and sang for the popular 1970s rock band Chicago. Though his band's music was popular, Kath was thought by his peers to be wildly underrated. Jimi Hendrix once reportedly named Kath as one of his favorite guitar players. If you want to hear how good he was, listen to the solo in Chicago's classic track "25 or 6 to 4."

Unfortunately, like Johnny Ace, Kath died young; also like Johnny Ace, it was due to an unfortunate accident with a firearm. Kath, who was known as something of a gun aficionado, was playing around with a 9mm which he believed was unloaded, and he jokingly he put the gun to his head and pulled the trigger, bringing an extremely promising career to a tragic end. His last words:

"Don't worry about it... Look, the clip is not even in it."

MARVIN GAYE (1939–1984)

There are few voices smoother than that of Marvin Gaye, and he could sing it all. Gaye's memorable hits range from the funky "I Heard It through the Grapevine" to the inspirational duet "Ain't No Mountain High Enough" to the sensual "Let's Get It On" and "Sexual Healing," to the hard-hitting social commentary of "What's Going On" and "Mercy Mercy Me." Gaye was a rare artist who could create classics for any decade, but sadly his career only spanned parts of three.

Gaye never get along with his father, who was a minister and a disciplinarian who lived by the old credo of spare the rod, spoil the child. When Marvin came home to help his ailing mother, he found himself in the middle of fights between his parents, and a lifetime of enmity came to a boil. On the night of his death, Marvin had enough of his father yelling at his mother and things came to blows before Marvin Senior pulled a gun on his son and pulled the trigger.

There are conflicting reports regarding his last words. The first apparently come from the moment before his father walked into the bedroom:

"I'm going to get my things and get out of this house. Father hates me, and I'm never coming back."

The second and more telling account comes from Gaye's brother Frankie, who says that at the end of his life, Marvin whispered to him:

"I got what I wanted... I couldn't do it myself, so I had him do it... It's good, I ran my race, there's no more left in me."

JIMI HENDRIX (1942–1970)

Jimi was born to play guitar. It was all he thought about for years before he bought his first real guitar for five dollars when he was fifteen years old. And once he had his hands on one, all bets were off. He would of course go on to reinvent what it meant to play.

Listening to Hendrix is like listening to the best pieces of classical music. He was a master of his instrument, understanding everything it could do and then pushing it to places it was never meant to go. He was controlled and experimental at the same time. He could improvise like the greats of jazz, using every sonic trick in the book. The driving blues of "Hey Joe," the hustle and bustle of "Crosstown Traffic," the complex beauty of "Bold as Love"—Jimi could do it all. And when he used his guitar to sonically scream the notes of "The Star-Spangled Banner," complete with rockets flaring and bombs dropping, Woodstock and the entire world stood up and took notice.

Sadly, like his contemporary visionaries Janis Joplin and Jim Morrison, Jimi died at only twenty-seven due to complications from drug use. His literal last words were, "I need help bad, man." But the more poetic last words come from a piece of writing found at his bedside at the time of his death:

"The story of life is quicker than the blink of an eye. The story of love is hello and goodbye. Until we meet again."

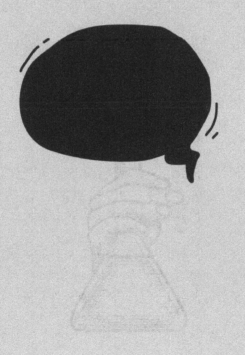

CHAPTER EIGHT

SCIENTISTS

It has been said that death is the greatest experiment of all, which is of course not really true as the outcome is pretty much set in stone. Well, not really, since the outcome is pretty much set in stone. One of the primary edicts of science is to repeat experiments, and, in the billions of times people have died, it has turned out more or less the same.

However, for anyone that dedicates their life to asking the hard questions and searching for the big answers, death must be pretty interesting, even if you would rather it was happening to someone else. Below is a collection of a few of the greatest minds the world has ever seen; these are the men and women that helped shape the forward progress of humanity. People who weren't afraid to ask questions and seek truth. Now they know the greatest truth of all.

SIR ISAAC NEWTON (1643–1727)

Newton is best known for developing the law of universal gravity, which would be enough on its own to solidify his place as one of history's greatest minds, but it is just the tip of the iceberg. His Laws of Motion laid the foundation for modern physics. His invention of a new type of math we now call calculus is integral to engineering and science. His contributions to the telescope made it possible to see further beyond our world than ever before.

Sir Isaac is as important to making the modern world as anyone in history, but unlike that famous apple, his greatness never got to his head. Newton was almost as famous for his humility as for his mind. A few of his oft-quoted lines include "If I have seen further than others, it is by standing upon the shoulders of giants," and "Tact is the knack of making a point without making an enemy."

Newton died in his sleep at the age of eighty-four. His last recorded words beautifully capture both his humility and his endless wonder:

"I don't know what I may seem to the world. But as to myself I seem to have been only like a boy playing on the seashore and diverting myself now and then in finding a smoother pebble or a prettier shell than the ordinary, whilst the great ocean of truth lay all undiscovered before me."

Thomas Fantet de Lagny (1660–1734)

Best known for calculating pi to 120 decimal places, which, when he did it in 1719, was an incredibly difficult and noteworthy feat, even if, as it turns out, he had eight of them incorrect. His record stood for seventy years until Jurij Vega made it all the way to 126 digits. As you can plainly see, the early days of competitive pi-calculating were edge-of-your-seat nail biters.

Lagny's life revolved around mathematics. He taught mathematics, he wrote papers about mathematics, in later life he was paid to study mathematics at the French Academy of Sciences. He was still doing math right up until his dying breath. When, on his deathbed, someone asked him what the square of 12 was, he answered:

"144."

RICHARD FEYNMAN (1918–1988)

Feynman truly lived a fascinating life. His work in the realm of quantum mechanics and quantum electrodynamics earned him a shared Nobel Prize in Physics. He helped lay the groundwork for nanotechnology. He was one of the brilliant minds tasked with helping to create the atomic bomb as part of Oppenheimer's Manhattan Project during World War II. He was also on the panel that investigated the Space Shuttle Challenger disaster. On top of all of this, he was a talented lecturer and writer and helped to popularize physics.

He was also one heck of a personality. Stories about Feynman are a dime a dozen in the science community. He tried his hand at art and acting, he used a topless bar as an office, he cracked safes for fun, he proudly never brushed his teeth. In short, he was the poster boy for the stereotype of the eccentric, but charming scientist.

Feynman has gone on to become a frequent subject of pop culture, being portrayed in several plays and films, including notable performances from Alan Alda and William Hurt. His last words:

"I'd hate to die twice. It's so boring."

CHARLES DARWIN (1809–1882)

The history of science is filled with huge moments, realizations that rocked the world and pulled back the curtain to show us a bit more of the universe. Few of these opened our eyes like the 1859 publication of Charles Darwin's *On the Origin of Species*. Darwin's theory of evolution and the process of natural selection shook the world.

It is difficult to overstate the importance of Darwin's work or how radical his ideas were at the time. His assertions were met by resistance from the quarters one might expect, but Darwin welcomed the debate openly, and, by the 1870s, the vast majority of the educated world had come to understand Darwin's assertions and accept them as fact. Today Darwin's discoveries are the foundation for how we understand life.

Darwin is buried in Westminster Abbey alongside fellow world-changer Sir Isaac Newton. His last words were:

"I am not the least afraid to die."

ALBERT A. MICHELSON (1853–1931)

The first American to be awarded the Nobel Prize in Physics was actually only kind of American. He was in fact born in Germany and moved to the states at age two.

In his early years, Michelson served in the US Navy, both on the high seas and as a professor of physics and chemistry in the US Naval Academy. Michelson's work crossed a number of disciplines, but he is perhaps most famous for his work measuring the speed of light, as well as being the first to measure the diameter of a star that was not the sun.

Michelson worked tirelessly throughout his life, earning a trophy case worth of awards recognizing his contributions. His last words came while doing what he loved:

"The following is a report on the measurement of the velocity of light made at the Irvine Ranch, near Santa Ana, California, during the period of September 1929 to—"

MARIE CURIE (1867–1934)

Madame Curie was the first person to be awarded two Nobel Prizes and is still the only person to be awarded a Nobel Prize in two different sciences. Her first Nobel Prize, in physics alongside her husband and their colleague, recognized her groundbreaking work with radiation. Her second, in chemistry, was awarded for several important discoveries, including that of radium.

Even though Curie battled sexism and xenophobia throughout her life, she remained steadfast in her drive.

After her death, she became the first woman to be entombed in the Pantheon on her own merits. Today she lies alongside her husband and France's greatest citizens.

Sadly, her discoveries would lead to her death. Unaware of the dangers of her work with radioactive materials, Curie battled illness for years before dying of leukemia at only fifty-seven. Her last words came as she was offered something for her pain:

"*Je ne le veux pas.*"

("I do not want it.")

ARCHIMEDES (287–212 BC)

Archimedes was a mathematician, inventor, engineer, astronomer, and physicist before some of these things were even things. It is difficult to overstate how far ahead of his time Archimedes was; he discovered the laws of levers and pulleys as well as the concept of the center of gravity. He was the first to calculate many of the equations we use today to figure out area and volume; he also invented all nature of things, including an enhanced system to pump water and a giant claw that pulled enemy ships out of the sea. To many at the time, Archimedes must have seemed like a wizard.

The great historian Plutarch suggests that Archimedes was killed in a siege of Syracuse. He was stabbed after he insisted on finishing a difficult mathematics problem rather than going to meet the conquering general, Marcus Claudius Marcellus. Plutarch doesn't mention Archimedes's last words, but they have been passed down through time nonetheless, though their origins and legitimacy are highly disputed:

"Do not disturb my circles."

THOMAS EDISON (1847–1941)

Edison is one of history's most controversial figures. While he was no doubt a talented inventor in his own right, it is difficult to distinguish which works belonged to Edison and which were a product of his large team of researchers and employees. Edison was the first to truly turn inventing into not just a business, but a huge corporation. He has been credited with important inventions in mining, illumination, sound, communication, electricity, medical diagnostics, motion pictures, and more.

Edison first garnered worldwide attention with his invention of the phonograph; from there, he went on to improve on several recent inventions by contemporaries before focusing on direct current. Edison was an incredibly competitive businessman. During the war of the currents, which he eventually lost to former employee Nikola Tesla's alternating current, Edison famously used publicity stunts, such as electrocuting a live elephant, as an attempt to frighten people away from his competitor.

Edison died of complication from diabetes. His last words came as he emerged briefly from a coma:

"It is very beautiful over there."

CHAPTER NINE

CRIMINALS

It is fitting that, when it comes to last words, criminals often cheat. This is especially true for anyone who is on death row. If you give someone weeks or months to work on a last line, chances are they can come up with a doozy. If anything, it's surprising that there aren't more zingers. There couldn't be a harder audience, but, whether it's sitting on the chair, lined up against a wall, or waiting for the bottom to drop out, these fellas took a crack at one more joke before literally dying on stage.

THOMAS B. MORAN (DIED 1971)

Died after a years-long career as an incredibly successful pickpocket. Apparently, Thomas was not thrilled with the nickname given to him in the local papers:

"I've never forgiven that smart-alecky reporter who named me Butterfingers. To me, it's not funny."

JAMES W. RODGERS (DIED 1960)

Sentenced to death for murder. While standing in front of a firing squad, Rodgers was asked if he had a last request. He did:

"A bulletproof vest."

CHARLES "LUCKY" LUCIANO (DIED 1962)

The man known as the father of organized crime in the US died of a heart attack just after a meeting with film producer Martin Golsch. His last words would prove to be prophetic, as he later became the subject of countless films:

"Tell Georgie I want to get in the movies one way or another."

THOMAS J. GRASSO (DIED 1995)

Sentenced to death in Oklahoma, a double murderer's elaborate final meal was missing one key ingredient, which apparently was still on his mind in his final hours:

"I did not get my Spaghetti-O's; I got spaghetti. I want the press to know this."

CARL PANZRAM (DIED 1930)

A particularly horrible person, who committed countless crimes over the course of his life. In his last moments he spat on his hangman and, when asked for last words, said:

"Hurry up, you Hoosier bastard. I could kill ten men while you're fooling around!"

JAMES FRENCH (DIED 1966)

French, a multiple murderer, was put to death in the electric chair. While his last words are disputed, it is commonly accepted that they were:

"Hey, fellas! How about this for a headline for tomorrow's paper? 'French Fries.' "

TOM "BLACK JACK" KETCHUM (DEATH 1901)

A Wild West outlaw, train robber, and member of the famed Hole in the Wall Gang, which also included Butch Cassidy and the Sundance Kid, Black Jack was executed by hanging in a county that had never hung anyone before. Apparently, he grew impatient, leading to a pair of reported last words:

"Goodbye. Please dig my grave very deep. All right; hurry up" or "I'll be in hell before you start breakfast. Let her rip!"

GEORGE APPEL (DIED 1928)

Sentenced to death by electric chair for murder. Appel reportedly went out with a pun:

"Well, gentlemen, you are about to see a baked Appel."

Francis "Two Gun" Crowley (Died 1932)

Executed at age nineteen, after a three-month crime spree that included several murders and a shoot-out with police, Crowley has two reported sets of last words. The first report is that he asked the warden for a rag to wipe the chair; his former partner in crime had been executed shortly before him: "I want to wipe off the chair after this rat sat in it." The second, more colorful, account suggests that the last thing he yelled at those present before he died was:

"You sons of bitches. Give my love to my mother."

CHAPTER TEN

Miscellaneous

Some people defy categories; they are true individuals, groundbreakers, mavericks. These are the adventurers, activists, magicians, and clairvoyants. Sometimes they are in slightly less romantic professions like economists and linguists. And sometimes they are in categories that are maybe not populated enough to warrant a whole section in a book. Either way, these folks were important, or had interesting enough last words, to include regardless of their difficult-to-categorize professions.

Let the breadth of careers in this section be a reminder that no matter what work you do, you will die. Unlike Nostradamus, you probably won't know when or how, so best to treat every sentence like it could be your last.

JOHN MAYNARD KEYNES (1883–1946)

This British economist has been described as one of the most influential economists of the twentieth century. His work helped to change international practices. He wrote extensively, including perhaps his best-known work, *The General Theory of Employment, Interest and Money.* Today his theories are widely used and known as Keynesian economics.

Interestingly, one of Keynes's core beliefs was that the point of building wealth was to provide for leisure. He was against the gathering of wealth for its own sake and argued for more holidays and a shorter work week.

When Keynes died of a heart attack at his home at the age of sixty-two, his last words were:

"I wish I'd drunk more champagne."

KIT CARSON (1809-1888)

Kit Carson was a legendary figure of westward expansion and the American frontier. Tales of Carson's exploits traveled far and wide during his lifetime. Carson was famous for his cool resolve under pressure, and the American public gobbled up stories of his combat prowess and fearlessness.

Dime-store novels of the time painted Carson as a near superhero, exaggerating his exploits and adventures. The stories sold across the world, making Carson one of the faces of the romanticized American frontier. While these stories glorified Carson's battles with Native Americans, he would later spend much of his time among indigenous people and argue their case in Washington.

In later life, Carson retired to a ranch in Colorado, where he lived with his wife and kids. He passed away just a month after the death of his wife who died from complications during pregnancy. His last words are an example of the exaggerations of the stories surrounding his life. Popular legend suggests that his last words were "I just wish I had time for one more bowl of chili." The more reliable account suggests that his last words were in fact:

"Goodbye, friends. *Adios, compadres.*"

EDWARD R. MURROW (1908–1965)

His is the first name to come to mind in any discussion of journalistic ethics. During his years in television and radio news broadcasting, Murrow made a name for himself as an impeccable beacon of truth and fairness.

Murrow was a fearless and honest war journalist and regularly reported from London during the Blitz. But his well-deserved reputation was solidified when he refused to back down from communist witch-hunter Senator Joseph McCarthy.

Sadly, Murrow died of lung cancer at age fifty-seven after reportedly smoking roughly three packs of Camels a day. His last words were to his wife:

"Well, Jan, we were lucky at that."

GILES COREY (1611–1692)

Corey is perhaps the most famous victim of the Salem witch trials, which were led by Puritan Christians in colonial Massachusetts. After he and his wife were arrested on charges of witchcraft, Corey was tortured in an attempt to force a guilty plea.

His accusers laid a board on his back and piled heavy rocks on top, though they underestimated their victim's resolve. After two days, all Corey's accusers could get from him each time they asked for a plea was a cry of "more weight." By refusing to take part, Corey ensured that his children would still have rights to his land. The brutality of his murder is also said to have been one of the key events that restored some sanity to the region.

The scene is famously dramatized in Arthur Miller's play *The Crucible*, which it seems remained fairly close to the facts of the "trial," including Corey's last words:

"More weight."

ROBERT ERSKINE CHILDERS (1870–1922)

Famous as both an author and an Irish Nationalist, his book *The Riddle of the Sands* was a popular pre-war adventure and spy novel. While his writing was influential, Childers is perhaps even better known for his part in the Irish Civil War, which would later lead to his arrest and subsequent execution.

Childers was executed by firing squad, but, before his sentence was carried out, he shook the hand of every man tasked with his execution before taking his mark and saying his famous final words:

"Take a step or two forward lads, it'll be easier that way."

HARRIET TUBMAN (1822–1913)

Born into slavery, Tubman escaped when she was twenty-seven and spent the rest of her life fighting injustice. After gaining her own freedom, Tubman continuously put herself in danger as she worked with the Underground Railroad to save others. In all, Tubman saved more than seventy people from slavery, risking her life over more than a dozen expeditions.

Tubman was as smart as she was tough, and she was extremely tough. One story states that when Tubman was undergoing a medical procedure that involved cutting open her skull, she refused anesthesia, choosing instead to bite down on a bullet.

Her small stature and unthreatening appearance helped her move undetected, but her quick thinking helped her get out of sticky situations. None of the people she shepherded from slavery were ever captured. Along with fighting the extreme racial injustice in the United States, Tubman was also a staunch advocate for the women's suffrage movement.

Tubman was ninety-one years old when she died of pneumonia, her last words:

"Swing low, sweet chariot."

HARRY HOUDINI (1874–1926)

Harry Houdini was the world's best-known escape artist. The Hungarian-born magician and escapologist began his career escaping from handcuffs, leg irons, and jail cells, which was impressive on its own, but this soon snowballed into straitjackets, water-filled chambers, and being buried alive among other death-defying stunts. After the death of his mother, Houdini became interested in mediums and spiritualism, which lead to him researching and ultimately debunking many who claimed to have paranormal abilities.

In order to perform his feats, Houdini had to train himself to endure extreme situations; this included strength, endurance, and training to hold his breath for up to four minutes. He was proud of his physical prowess and bragged that he could withstand punches to his abdomen, a claim that would haunt him. After a show in Montreal, a university student asked him about his debunking of religious "miracles" as well as his claim that he could take any punch. After Houdini said the latter was true, the man punched him several times without warning. Just days after this incident, after performing a pair of shows through pain and fever, Houdini would die of a ruptured appendix. His last words:

"I'm tired of fighting."

JACK DANIEL (1850–1911)

Born in Lynchburg, Tennessee, Jack Daniel has become perhaps the most famous distiller in the world. Daniel began working in a distillery at a young age and learned the ins and outs of the process from a man named "Nearest" Green. Green was a slave at the time but was later emancipated, and he and several of his sons would go on to work at Jack Daniel Distillery. The distillery later officially naming Green the first master distiller in the company's history.

The first big break for Jack Daniel's Tennessee Whiskey came when it was awarded a gold medal at the 1904 St. Louis World's Fair. The brand is now a household name and is sold around the world. Ironically, the distillery's home county has apparently been dry since Prohibition.

Daniel died of blood poisoning in 1911; his last words were:

"One last drink, please."

NOSTRADAMUS (1503–1566)

History's most famous prognosticator, Nostradamus is best known as the writer of *Les Propheties*. Some think that the 942 poetic quatrains have correctly predicted all nature of important events; others think they are the purposefully vague work of a charlatan.

No matter which side of the debate one falls on, it seems that one thing Nostradamus did correctly prophesize was his own death. According to his secretary, the last thing Nostradamus said the evening before he was found dead was:

"Tomorrow, at sunrise, I shall no longer be here."

AMELIA EARHART (1897–1937)

The fearless aviator was the first woman to fly solo across North America and back, the first woman to fly solo across the Atlantic, and the first aviator of any gender to fly from Honolulu to Oakland. These were just a few of her many, many impressive feats of aviation, as Earhart quickly became an international sensation.

Sadly, on July 2, 1937, Earhart would depart for her last flight, before mysteriously vanishing in the central Pacific Ocean. Her disappearance continues to be a hotly debated topic of significant interest today, with theories including a crash at sea, death on a deserted island, capture by Japanese forces, and even an elaborate plot to escape the limelight and change her identity.

Her final transmission was:

"We are running on line north and south."

CHAPTER ELEVEN

TOMBSTONES

As we have established, getting your last words just right is extremely difficult. Even if you have a plan, there is no guarantee you will have a chance to execute it. A few clever celebs have found a way around that. These men and women thought ahead and had their final words inscribed on their tombstones. There is no better way to get the last laugh then to carve it into granite.

MERV GRIFFIN (1925–2007)

Singer, actor, producer, and host—you probably know him best as the creator of *Jeopardy* and *Wheel of Fortune* and host of *The Merv Griffin Show*. You might not know that he also scored a 1950s hit with the song "I've Got a Lovely Bunch of Coconuts."

His epitaph:

"I will *not* be right back after this message."

MEL BLANC (1908–1989)

He was the man of a thousand voices. If you had a favorite cartoon character from *Looney Tunes*, chances are it was voiced by Mel Blanc. Bugs, Daffy, Porky, Tweety, Sylvester, Sam, Marvin, Pepe Le Pew: they were all Blanc. It was basically a one-man show. He is even credited with the Road Runner's *meep*s and Wile E's sounds of distress.

There was really only one thing that could go on his tombstone:

"That's All Folks."

JACK LEMMON (1925–2001)

One of the best straight men in the business, Lemmon is probably best known for his work with Walter Matthau as the tidy half of *The Odd Couple*, and the slightly less grumpy one in *Grumpy Old Men*. These are just a small sample from Lemmon's impressive filmography, which also includes *Some Like It Hot*, *The Apartment*, *Glengarry Glen Ross*, and an Oscar-winning role in *Mister Roberts*. Lemmon racked up almost one hundred acting credits in his fifty years as one of the most beloved actors in Hollywood.

Lemmon's tombstone looks a lot like a billing for his final film:

"Jack Lemmon in..."

BILLY WILDER (1906–2002)

When it came to film in the 1950s and '60s, nobody could touch Billy Wilder. A clever director and an all-but-perfect writer, Wilder could do everything from mystery to comedy. Between *Double Indemnity*, *Sunset Boulevard*, *The Apartment*, *The Spirit of St. Louis*, and *Some Like It Hot*, Wilder's resume is basically a greatest hits list of classic films.

Wilder's characters often had a clever, self-deprecating charm, as does his tombstone:

"I'm a writer but then nobody's perfect."

ROBERT CLAY ALLISON (1841–1887)

Confederate soldier, gunfighter, and rancher who once rode through town wearing only a gun belt, Allison was known as a disagreeable man who was quick enough with a gun to come out on the alive side of several showdowns.

His epitaph:

"He never killed a man that did not need killing."

DOC HOLLIDAY (1851–1887)

Gambler, drinker, gunfighter, dentist, and good friend of Wyatt Earp, Doc Holliday's legend has continued to grow since his death. Holliday has become famous through books and film, usually depicted as a roguish gentleman with a quick wit and a calm demeanor. The man who fought alongside Earp has more than a few classic lines attributed to him, including the oh-so-cool "I'm your Huckleberry." It is fitting that both his last words and his epitaph contain the subtle charm he has become famous for.

Last words: "This is funny."

Epitaph: "He died in bed."

RODNEY DANGERFIELD (1921–2004)

The man who famously got no respect was an enormous talent with an equally enormous heart. There was and is nobody better at the self-deprecating one-liner. Dangerfield had one for every occasion, and they were tear-the-house-down zingers. Star of stage and screen, Dangerfield also ran a New York-based venue that helped launch a who's who of comedy greats.

His tombstone perfectly encapsulates his trademark wit:

"There goes the neighborhood."

LESLIE NIELSEN (1926-2010)

This Canadian legend may have started his career as a handsome leading man in films such as *Forbidden Planet*, but he will forever be remembered for his great comedic turns in classics such as *Airplane!* and *The Naked Gun*. The actor's love of the simple pleasures of a whoopee cushion gag or a fart joke is captured perfectly on his tombstone:

"Let 'er rip."

PATRICIA NIXON (1912–1993)

Say what you want about her husband, but Pat Nixon was one smart and tough lady, even if she hid it under a quiet charm. Even after her husband's less than favorable exit from office, Pat remained one of America's most respected women. Today she remains cast in a largely positive light, due to both her inspiring rags-to-riches story and the many tales of her general warmth and kindness.

Her epitaph reads:

"Even when people can't speak your language, they can tell if you have love in your heart."

WILLIAM BUTLER YEATS (1865–1939)

The great Irish poet and winner of the Nobel Prize in Literature left the world with an impressive list of phenomenal works, "Leda and the Swan," "Sailing to Byzantium," "Easter, 1916," and "The Second Coming," just to name a few. His words will surely be immortalized for generations to come, including the three lines found on his tombstone which were taken from one of his final poems:

"Cast a cold Eye

On Life, on Death.

Horseman, pass by."

BETTE DAVIS (1908–1989)

One of the greatest actresses in Hollywood history, Davis played every kind of role there was, and she shone in all of them. Her larger-than-life presence on the screen mirrored her tough persona off camera. Bette Davis may have been a woman in a man's world, but she wasn't about to shut up and play the game. Davis could go toe-to-toe with anyone, and her tombstone echoes the way she proudly lived her life:

"She did it the hard way."

CALAMITY JANE (1852–1903)

Despite her being one of the most famous women of the Wild West, not much is known about the life of Martha Jane Canary outside of her own stories and her time in *Deadwood*. Many of the biggest points of contention about her life revolve around her relationship with Wild Bill Hickok whom, depending on who you ask, either didn't care much for her or married her in secret. Regardless of what her relationship was with Hickok, we know that her final request both was honored and would become her epitaph:

"Bury me beside Wild Bill."

PETER FALK (1927–2011)

Whether it's in his roles in classic comedies like *It's a Mad, Mad, Mad, Mad World* and *Murder by Death*, his fantastic turn as *Columbo*, or skipping over the kissing parts as the grandpa in *The Princess Bride*, we all love Peter Falk. Very few actors have the everyman charm or blue-collar wisdom of Falk. He is buried in Los Angeles next to his wife, who is the subject of his touching epitaph:

"I'm not here. I'm home with Shera."

DEAN MARTIN (1917–1995)

You don't get much cooler than Dean Martin. The crooner and comedy straight man had an effortless charm and smooth voice that made him one of the best-loved performers of his generation. Martin did it all as part of the Rat Pack, one half of the great Martin and Lewis, and a sensation in his own right, with signature songs like "Ain't That a Kick in the Head, and You're Nobody till Somebody Loves You." One of his best-loved singles also serves as a touching epitaph:

"Everybody loves somebody sometime."

JIM MORRISON (1943–1971)

The Doors' front man has one of the most popular gravesites in the world, still frequented by his legion of fans who take the pilgrimage to Pere Lachaise Cemetery in Paris, France. Morrison's resting place has been anything but restful. Originally the singer's grave was unmarked before a bust was placed on the site and then stolen, leading to a second bust and a bronze marker, neither of which are at the actual gravesite. The current marker was placed in 1990 with text chosen by his father, written in Greek. The epitaph roughly translates as:

"True to his own spirit."

MARCEL DUCHAMP (1887–1968)

There are not many artists that have had the impact of the revolutionary Marcel Duchamp. The French-American painter and sculptor pushed the ideas of art to new and often absurd heights. While Duchamp was an incredibly talented painter, he is best known for his Dadaist pieces. His work was sometimes playful, often controversial, and almost always groundbreaking. Like much of his work, Duchamp's epitaph has a touch of humor hidden below the surface:

"D'ailleurs, c'est toujours les autres qui meurent."

("Besides, it's always the others who die.")

A Few More Last Words

Remember when you were a kid and people's moms would tell them to always wear clean underwear, because you never know if you would get hit by a bus? What moms probably should say is, be careful what you say, because every sentence could be your last. Admittedly, that would be a terrifying thing for a kid to hear, but it is good advice nonetheless. Wikipedia doesn't add a note for the clever thing you said on the third Wednesday of March, or that nice thing you said last week. Last words are different; they matter, as you have seen in the pages preceding this one.

However, a life well lived goes a long way to getting them right. The luckiest among us get to go out with an "I love you"—although Oscar Wilde's crack about the wallpaper is a pretty close second. If there is a lesson in this book, it is that we tend to die as we live. So we have two choices—live well or don't die. The first one is probably easier.

Though I wouldn't worry too much, most of us will die in our sleep. But of course, we don't know what night will be our last. Isn't that reassuring?

Good night.

ABOUT THE AUTHOR

Joseph Hayden is a collector of words, experiences, and all things esoterica. He has lived on five continents, including a five month stay on Antarctica, and has visited thirty-five countries to date. He currently lives in the Rocky Mountains with his wife, Joan, and their secretly intelligent golden retriever, Seamus Finnigan. He is an avid reader, a passing dancer, and has regrettably been known to speak while brushing his teeth on more than one occasion. *Any Last Words?* is his first book.